Love Signs
🔲 *for beginners* 🔲

LOVE SIGNS

KRISTYNA ARCARTI

A catalogue record for this title is available from The British Library

ISBN 0 340 648058

First published 1995
Impression number 10 9 8 7 6 5 4 3 2 1
Year   1999 1998 1997 1996 1995

Copyright © 1995 Kristyna Arcarti

All rights reserved. No part of this publication may be reproduced or transmitted in any form or by any means, electronic or mechanical, including photocopy, recording, or any information storage and retrieval system, without permission in writing from the publisher or under licence from the Copyright Licensing Agency Limited. Further details of such licences (for reprographic reproduction) may be obtained from the Copyright Licensing Agency Limited, of 90 Tottenham Court Road, London, W1P 9HE.

Typeset by Transet Limited, Coventry, England
Printed in Great Britain for Hodder & Stoughton Educational, a division of Hodder Headline plc, 338 Euston Road, London NW1 3BH by Cox and Wyman Limited, Reading.

For Beginners

This series of books is written for the growing number of people who, disillusioned with the sterility of our technological age, are looking to traditional, esoteric arts to find out more about themselves and others.

Other books in the series include:

Tarot for Beginners
Star Signs for Beginners
Palmistry for Beginners
Numerology for Beginners
Gems and Crystals for Beginners
Graphology for Beginners
Dowsing for Beginners
Feng Shui for Beginners
Chakras for Beginners
I Ching for Beginners
Meditation for Beginners
Visualisation for Beginners
Chinese Horoscopes for Beginners

CONTENTS

INTRODUCTION	1

Chapter 1 Our Love Lives	**3**
Using the information	4
How astrology works	4
Looking at relationships	5
The importance of the Moon	8
The Moon through the ages	9
Finding our Moon sign	12
The other planets	12
Linking it all together	17

Chapter 2 Moon Placements	**20**
Aries	20
Taurus	23
Gemini	26
Cancer	30
Leo	33
Virgo	36
Libra	39
Scorpio	41
Sagittarius	44
Capricorn	48
Aquarius	50
Pisces	53

Chapter 3	Moon and Sun signs	57
Aries		58
Taurus		60
Gemini		62
Cancer		63
Leo		65
Virgo		66
Libra		68
Scorpio		69
Sagittarius		71
Capricorn		73
Aquarius		74
Pisces		76

Chapter 4	Compatibility	79
Sun sign compatibility		79
Moon and Sun sign compatibility		81

Appendix	Finding Moon signs	95

Further reading		117

INTRODUCTION

Most of us are deeply interested in our love lives, whether we have a current relationship or not.

In my work helping people through astrology and other esoteric forms, I've found that 90 per cent of people ask for help with their love lives and 10 per cent for help in career matters. Most either have a problem in their relationship, haven't got a relationship and want to find one, or have just come out of a relationship and are seeking guidance on how to go forwards on their own. You may be in one of those situations, or you may be in a happy relationship yet want to understand your partner a little better. This book aims to help by showing you how to interpret the Moon placement in your natal chart and in the charts of partners.

Relationships come in many guises, and go through many stages. Sometimes there is a friendship which blossoms into something more. Sometimes there is an initial attraction and the relationship moves quickly into something passionate and deep. Unfortunately at other times love is not reciprocated, or a bond is broken.

The Moon placement in your natal chart gives information on your emotional nature. It is just as important as your general character information, covered in *Star Signs for Beginners*, but it shows your softer and more personal side. Venus and Mars also give information on your emotional nature, as does the rising sign or Ascendant, which gives us information about how other people see us and about the way in which we are initially attracted to people. We will, however, concentrate on the Moon placement.

It is relatively easy to discover your Moon placement. This achieved, we can then explore questions about the type of person or people you are likely to be attracted to, and identify your emotional needs and how this relates to your star sign, as well as other issues concerning what makes you the person you are. As we progress, we will explore compatibilities, our emotional make-up, and areas where potential problems could occur.

Everybody should find something in this book for them. Irrespective of age, whether you are gay or straight, married, co-habiting or single and looking for that special person, you will find this book informative and fun.

An astrologer's main aim is to help people understand themselves a little better, because only if we understand ourselves can we ever hope to form strong relationships.

In an ideal world, all relationships would blossom, and everybody would find that special someone who loves them for what they are, and whom they can love in return. This book could help you in that search, although it doesn't take away your personal responsibility, your inner voice, which goes to make you the unique person you really are.

OUR LOVE LIVES

We are about to set out on a voyage of discovery. As with any journey, there is more than one possible destination, route and mode of transport. Moreover, we may choose to stop off at several places before deciding on our final destination.

This is what normally happens in a person's life – we have several relationships, some more meaningful and lasting than others, before we finally settle on the 'ultimate destination'. For the purposes of this book, our goal is to discover more about our love lives, and our main means of travel is the Moon placement in our zodiac chart. This book can be seen as our travel brochure. However, as most seasoned travellers will know, you can only judge whether you will like the destination by going there yourself!

Most people want to know if they are compatible with others. There are at least three reasons for this. Maybe they have just met somebody and need to know whether the relationship is likely to work or not; maybe they need confirmation of their feelings about an existing relationship; or maybe there is nobody special in their lives and they would like an indication of the type of person they are likely to get on well with. It is important to try to understand yourself before even contemplating involvement with somebody else.

Few people really understand themselves, let alone the people who share their lives. It is therefore a good idea to use this book to understand yourself better before moving on to look at the object of your desire.

Using the information

I would never advise anyone to decide their marital future by means of this or any other book, whether using astrology or any other method. Each person is totally unique. From an astrological perspective, this is owing to the interplay of the planets and zodiac, which have a bearing on who and what we are, how we react, and how we interrelate.

It would be ludicrous to suggest that a person's whole future should revolve around their astrological chart. Such things are there to instruct and guide us, but not to dictate our every move. I believe firmly in free will, and also in personal responsibility, but we are more able to exercise these once we discover our true emotional self. We often try to hide things with which we are not comfortable. To understand ourselves and move forward, we need to uncover them.

How astrology works

Over the years, clients have asked me many questions, some demanding the best dates for separation, some merely asking if a relationship is likely to happen or prove satisfactory. My answers aren't always those hoped for, and I can hazard a guess that most astrologers will agree that, with the various techniques and systems for working out compatibilities, mistakes are bound to be made. Most astrologers would also agree that it is a difficult if not impossible task to predict actual dates in somebody's personal life.

When looking at a full natal chart (that means the chart showing all planet placements at the moment of birth), an astrologer can assess the emotional make-up of the person concerned. When assessing compatibility between two people, most astrologers will look first at the number of planets in each element in both charts. They will look at the Moon and Sun, and each of the planets, the Ascendant, Midheaven, Moon's nodes, and the aspects between planets and

angles in both charts. They will also look at the house placements. Love affairs are shown by what is know as the fifth house of our charts, and partnerships by the seventh house. The ninth house shows mutual contracts, the eighth shared resources, sexual love and feelings, the eleventh friendships, and so on. This can cause a lot of confusion, but looking at Moon placements is relatively straightforward. That does not mean that other factors should be ignored, but the Moon placement (like the Sun placement) is a strong indication of whether people are likely to get on or not. The Moon is the ruler of the fourth house. It influences home life, and travels through the zodiac each month.

Those interested in Chinese horoscopes (the subject of another book in this series) might like to know that the lunar mansions and Moon connections are as strong in the oriental system as they are in the Western. Likewise, the Moon has a strong connection with the I Ching (also covered by a book in this series), the Moon being yin and the Sun being yang, and students of tarot will know of the Major Arcana card The Moon.

Looking at Relationships

When thinking about relationships, it is a good idea to look initially at the individual's Sun sign, sometimes called the star sign or zodiac sign. Sun sign compatibilities are a strong factor in determining whether people are likely to get on or not. Readers of my *Star Signs for Beginners* will already be aware of the importance of the elements in compatibility. The fire signs – Aries, Leo and Sagittarius – normally relate well with one another. The same is true of the earth signs (Taurus, Virgo, Capricorn), the air signs (Gemini, Libra, Aquarius), and the water signs (Cancer, Scorpio, Pisces). So what happens when people from differing groups form a relationship?

Is is quite true in many cases that opposites attract, and an Aries can find a Libra very interesting, and so on through the signs. In much the same way as people from differing countries and backgrounds can get on well with each other, individuals from

LOVE SIGNS FOR BEGINNERS

different elements can get on well, but it is also necessary to see how the planets in the two natal charts interact. This is when the Moon, as well as the placement of the other planets, comes into play.

However, before we move on to that, thinking in terms of Sun or star sign only, the following rules generally apply. Two people of the same sign will know each other really well, probably too well, and this can lead to problems. Someone one sign ahead of you can help you move forward, whereas someone from the sign before you can often understand you quite deeply. Someone two signs ahead will be like a brother or sister to you, whereas someone two signs behind you will be a friend, or maybe just an acquaintance. The person three signs ahead of you will be a great ally to have in a conflict, whereas the person three signs back from you will be a good ally in material or business matters. The person four signs in front or behind you will be someone with whom you feel comfortable, but the relationship won't have any sparkle. Someone five signs ahead will help you no matter what, whereas the person five signs behind you will help you with ideas and possibly money. Your opposite sign is someone six signs either ahead or behind you, and will be your complement. Their strengths will be your weaknesses, and vice versa.

As most people will readily admit, two Aries people won't be exactly the same. One reason for this is that they probably won't have the same Moon placement. As a result their personalities will be very different.

As we know, there are four elements – earth, air, fire and water. We can look at these in the table on the next page and work out roughly whether we are likely to get on or not. Read across the page until you find the element for the male partner and then read down the page to find the element for the female partner; where the two meet you will find an assessment on their compatibility. Again I must point out that this is only a rough guide, and as we progress, we will learn far more detailed information about compatibilities.

OUR LOVE LIVES

MALE ▶ FEMALE ▼	EARTH	AIR	FIRE	WATER
EARTH	A good chance of success, but may be lacking in excitement. Lots of security.	Fun and interest but the earth sign may be too serious at times.	Difficult for both, as the fire sign needs more space.	Lots of security but not much sparkle.
AIR	Can work given time. Lots of stability but different types.	Great team who may have a problem with showing emotions.	Great. Lots of happy times and warmth.	Maybe. Needs a lot of care to survive.
FIRE	Volatile but could work. Fixed opinions will cause problems.	Lots of talk, little passion? Mutual attraction.	Exciting and emotional. Beware of burnout.	Prospects and passion. Moods can cause problems.
WATER	Security and love abound. Lots of support and understanding.	Maybe too many differences. Could work out but needs patience.	Initially OK but problems later on.	Sensitive loving and a great team.

The Importance of the Moon

Everybody will be aware of their Sun or star sign. You will know, then, that your Sun sign doesn't change, and that it forms the core of your personality. You are born under a certain zodiac sign, and you stay with it. Likewise, the position of the Moon in your chart doesn't alter, and neither do the positions of any of the planets.

The Moon passes through the zodiac in 28 days. The portion through which it passes in one day is known as a mansion. Therefore there are 28 lunar mansions, as anyone familiar with Chinese astrology will already know. Students of Chinese ways might also already know that the Chinese had a Moon goddess by the name of Shing-Moo. Scientists will argue that the Moon isn't a planet but a satellite. Astrologers and students of the esoteric will generally accept that the astral plane comes under the Moon's rulership, as do the unconscious mind, dreams and psychic sensitivities. It is said that a person's psychic powers are at their peak at the Full Moon, and that this is the best time for divination to take place. Many who practise divination will be aware of the practices of Full Moon divination, which are too complicated to go into here, but which use four coins, water and numbers, obtained by the throwing of the coins (very similar in many respects to the way of obtaining the hexagrams in the I Ching).

The Moon is connected with the unconscious desire of the individual and with instincts. It shows us our innermost needs and desires, and how we relate to ourselves as well as to others. It is also concerned with moods, memory, our emotional responses, empathy and sympathy.

The position of the Moon in your birth chart will show an astrologer how you will react to various experiences, how you may have been influenced by attitudes shown to you in childhood, and how your home life as an adult and your relationships with your family have been affected.

As the Moon controls the ebb and flow of the tides, it is also associated with the menstrual cycle in women, the human body being around 70 per cent water. The Moon is traditionally associated with the mother or wife, with the family as a unit, and with the regeneration of bodily cells.

The Moon through the ages

The Moon features in many ancient myths and legends. Indian myth saw Soma (the Moon) depicted as a horse, the Romans had a Moon goddess, Diana (Artemis to the Greeks) and it is said that the luck a horseshoe is supposed to bring is because the shape resembles the crescent moon. Possibly because the Moon was said to exert such an influence over people, the plant moonwort (honesty) was also a popular healing herb to people of days gone by.

Moon worship has existed since prehistoric times, and in biblical times there were many nations who actively practised such things. The Jews marked the New Moon by blowing trumpets and offering up sacrifices. Modern Judaism observes the New Moon of each month as a minor day of atonement for sins committed during the month just ended. The Sumerians had a Moon god, Sin, who was also the city god of Ur, although Moon worship centred on the town of Haran. The town of Ur should not be confused with the oriental Moon god and Assyrian fire god of the same name, although it is interesting that the orientals called their god by a name also used as a place name associated with Moon worship elsewhere.

Other biblical texts point to the habit at that time of kissing the hand to the Moon, the Midianites used Moon-shaped ornaments, and in Egypt Moon worship was prominently practised in honour of the Moon god Thoth, the Egyptian god of measures, wisdom and learning. At every Full Moon, the Egyptians sacrificed a pig to him. Biblical records show that in Canaan the worship of the Moon was via her goddess Ashtoreth. Moon worship did in fact at that time

LOVE SIGNS FOR BEGINNERS

extend all the way to the Western world, and ancient ziggurat temples dedicated to the Moon have been found in Mexico and Central America, the Aztecs having a Moon goddess by the name of Metztli. In England the Anglo-Saxon word 'Monday' stems from 'Moon Day'.

To mankind of old, the Moon's phases brought differing conditions. It was thought at one time that a Full Moon could make a woman pregnant, and as a result, women who wanted to become pregnant slept under the rays of the Full Moon. Similarly, in ancient times women used to go into Moon huts during menstruation to contemplate and absorb the power of the Moon.

The ancients soon realised that the Moon disappeared from the heavens to reappear, to grow again to full size. This they linked with rebirth and the dead, and Plutarch, a first-century Greek writer, suggested that the Moon was a stopping-off point for souls after death and prior to rebirth, a theme followed through by the ancient Celts. The Babylonians worshipped the Moon as the ancestor of the Sun.

Whilst it is generally accepted by Western students that the lunar force is passive and feminine, and lunar goddesses predominate over gods probably because of the female links with the Moon and its associations with the life force, this has not always been the case. The Egyptians once had a Moon god, Khensu, although they later had a Moon goddess, Isis, who had originally been an earth goddess. The Nordic peoples had Frey, as students of runes will know. Frey and his twin sister Freya were linked with the seasons and with fertility in much the same way as the Moon. Many aboriginal races still regard the Moon as a masculine force and legends refer to the god Bahloo. Many children will still be told stories and learn nursery rhymes about the Man in the Moon.

The Moon later became associated with witchcraft, magic and sorcery and witches still work closely with the Moon for healing spells, banishing spells and working against the forces of evil. The 13 Full Moons of the year still play an important role in pagan and Wiccan belief systems.

The word 'lunacy' comes from the word *luna* relating to the Moon, and meaning possessed by the spirit of the Greek goddess Luna. The term 'mania' is also derived from 'moon'. Other terms still in common use include 'moonstruck', and one theory suggests that the word 'month' was originally 'moonth' and was so called because of the lunar cycle of 28 days, a period close to a full month. It was thought for centuries that the Moon exercised some peculiar spell over people, and that they could become mad, hence probably the stories about werewolves who howled at the Moon. Many people attributed the disease of epilepsy to the Moon. Strange as it may seem, there may be a link between health and the Moon, and some medical professionals continue to study the effect it has on human behaviour.

Similarly, gardeners have long known that the Moon has an effect on a plant's intake of water, and crops have for many centuries been grown and harvested according to the lunar phases. Moisture absorption is said to be at its lowest with the New Moon, and as the moon waxes, a plant's intake of water increases, reaching its zenith at the time of the Full Moon. This is also linked to a plant's metabolic rate and growth cycle, which also reach a peak during the period of the Full Moon. Horticultarlists who study lunar phases say that vegetables picked at the New Moon when the water content of the plant is at its lowest are likely to store well, whereas those picked at Full Moon need to be eaten almost immediately and will not keep. Lunar gardening is a subject on its own, and there are many people who plant and grow bulbs and crops using lunar phases.

For many years I have been aware that people act somewhat differently during different phases of the Moon. I have a friend, for example, who is Cancerian (the Moon rules Cancer) and he is very temperamental around the time of a Full Moon, Cancerians naturally being far more sensitive to lunar phases than others. Likewise I am very affected by the Moon, and have noticed over the years that various phases of the Moon (again especially the Full Moon) regularly find me depressed and oversensitive, maybe because I am a Capricorn, the opposite sign to Cancer perhaps?

Having discovered this, I am a little more aware of how I am likely to react at certain times. The problem is explaining that to others!

Statistics suggest that there are more outbursts of violence, accidents and sexual crimes during a Full Moon than at other times. From a medical angle it is interesting to note that the cycle of human ovulation equals the length of the full lunar cycle, and that patients undergoing surgery are likely to lose more blood if operated on at the Full Moon, when blood seems to flow more freely.

As we have already discussed, the Moon features strongly in oriental astrology. In Hindu (Vedic) astrology the Moon placement takes precedence over the Sun as the ruling planet in a chart. This is because most people tend to act on their unconscious desires, which we have already seen relate to the Moon, rather than any objective reasoning, which relates to the Sun placement. The Hindu Moon goddess is known as Parvati.

Finding our Moon sign

The Sun sign is easy to explain and understand, and works around the same dates each month, but the Moon sign is a little more difficult to find. An ephemeris at the end of this book shows the position of the Moon at midnight on every other day, as the Moon changes sign approximately every two and a half days. Once you find your year, month and day of birth, you then look at the degrees shown in the ephemeris and from that you work out your Moon sign. Don't worry too much about that now. We will discuss it in more detail at the end of the book.

The other planets

As already mentioned, there are several planets which relate to our love lives. It is only right and proper for us to look at these, however briefly, before we embark on our main journey, as those readers

 our love lives

wishing to undertake further study need to be aware of the importance of all the planets. We will start by looking at Venus and Mars, which are the two main planets most astrologers will consider after the Moon and Sun placements, both having to do with attraction, love, sex and desire.

VENUS

Venus is the planet of romantic love, also known as the evening star, being the brightest planet. Interestingly, despite this connection with love and harmony, another name for the planet when it appears in the sky before sunrise is Lucifer! Venus lies between the Earth and Mercury, and takes 225 days to complete an orbit round the Sun. It governs feelings, relations, romantic ideals, comfort and beauty. Another female planet in essence, it is associated with values, passivity, the ability to attract others, with affection and harmony. This is the planet which unites, which evaluates and which brings about feeling, and represents our ability to attract and be attracted romantically to other people. Traditionally the placement of Venus in a man's chart shows the type of woman to whom he will be attracted sexually.

MARS

Mars, which takes its name from the Roman god of war, is the planet of initiatives and personal will, and concerns the initial starting point, the courage to get going, the sexual urge, desires and passions, as well as aggression. Seen essentially as a masculine planet, Mars also concerns the self or ego and the energy level of the individual and the amount of competitive spirit. The position of Mars in a woman's chart normally shows the type of man she will be attracted to and how she will respond sexually. Mars takes just over two years (687 days in fact) to travel through the houses of the birth chart.

JUPITER

♃

Jupiter is astronomically the largest planet. It takes 12 years to travel through the birth chart and is traditionally associated with wisdom, knowledge and material matters, being known as 'the Seer Planet', as it is said to enhance the ability for positive thought. This planet also concerns ethics, humour and the social side of life, as well as understanding, and is symbolic of expansion, growth and opportunities. Linked to the power of creative visualisation, a well-aspected Jupiter can lead to fulfilment in a relationship.

SATURN

♄

Another planet associated with wisdom, this is the planet of structure, which is needed in large amounts for relationships to succeed. It takes Saturn over 29 years to travel through the birth chart, thus spending 2½ years in each zodiac sign. Strongly

associated with marriage, the placement of Saturn in a chart concerns duty, commitment and responsibility. When looking at two natal charts, especially if the couple are married, an astrologer will play close attention to Saturn aspects. Emotional and material security, insecurities and fears are also associated with this planet, as is age, as Saturn concerns authority and status, which come with age. It also concerns restrictions.

URANUS

Uranus is the first of the so-called 'modern' planets. It was discovered in 1781. It is the planet of free will, freedom and independence, space and change, deviation and excitement, psychology, of breakdown or breakthrough. This planet, which takes on average 84 years to travel through the birth chart, and which moves into a new sign every seven years, often throws spanners in the works of otherwise seemingly compatible charts, relationships which flow one minute and stop the next, sudden boredom with a relationship or a need for more space, perhaps something like the seven-year itch!

Known as the planet of unexpected revelation, Uranus governs quick thinking and telepathic links with others of a like mind. Its placement can show unconventional relationships and transformation through change.

On average Uranus reaches a point opposite its original place in a person's chart when they are 42, a time when many people experience a 'midlife crisis'. However, the erratic orbit of Uranus means that currently this is affecting people at the age of 39.

MERCURY

The smallest and speediest planet in the solar system concerns communication (Mercury was messenger to the gods), without which most relationships are doomed to failure. How many times do you hear couples complaining that they seem unable to communicate? Even if a couple have a wonderful sex life, without proper communication the relationship is doomed to failure, or at the least to difficulties. It is important when looking at two natal charts for compatibility to take into account whether their Mercury placements are well aspected. Mercury is also representative of young men and ideas. Mercury is never more than 28 degrees away from the Sun, and each sign covers 30 degrees. Therefore Mercury will either be in the same sign as the Sun, or in the preceding or following one.

NEPTUNE

Neptune is the second of the 'modern' planets, discovered in 1846. It is the planet of devotion, unrequited or fantasy loves and confusion. Often seen as the planet of imagination and illusion at its utmost, this planet causes idealistic feelings to emerge, feelings of sensitivity and compassion, and also concerns the art of subtlety. It takes approximately 14 years to pass through a zodiac sign. Known as the planet of inspiration, imagination and the mystic arts, it is also concerned with what you sacrifice, how you react, or where you escape to in times of challenge or crisis and how creative you are likely to be, both inside and outside of a relationship. Neptune is probably the planet most closely associated with psychic ability, and its placement in a chart can indicate heightened sensitivities.

pluto

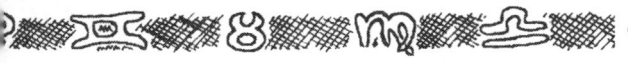

The most remote of our planets, and not observed until 1930, Pluto is concerned with make or break affairs, with perseverance and with relationships which either make us or destroy us completely, as it is also associated with jealousy and obsession. This planet is the planet of renewal or elimination, secrets and mystery, intensity and depth, or death and rebirth, and aids intuition and instincts. Pluto has a really strange orbit and spends as long as 30 years in some signs but as few as 13 in others.

Linking it all together

Let's use a real-life example here to help us understand how Moon placements fit into the scheme of things when looking at a person and their emotional or love life.

Lydia is a Capricorn. That means her Sun sign is Capricorn. This is going to give us information on her basic character. From the ephemeris at the back of this book, knowing her date of birth, we have found that she has her Moon in Taurus. This information is going to show her inner or emotional self. Let's further pretend that we have done extra calculations to find out what her Ascendant is. The Ascendant, or rising sign, is the starting point on a natal chart.

Picture the signs of the zodiac like a belt circling the earth, against which the earth revolves daily. The Ascendant or rising sign is the zodiac sign on the eastern horizon at the time of birth. Astrologically, the Ascendant shows the public face of the person – how other people see them, which isn't always their true self. Most of us, at times, put on a front, especially in business situations. We have looked up this information, and Lydia has a Virgo Ascendant. Another way of putting this would be to say that Lydia has Virgo rising.

Lydia's basic characteristics therefore are as follows.

Sun in Capricorn   Serious, moody at times and very ambitious, Lydia will stick at things, probably not show her emotions too much, and may be rather shy. With lots of hidden insecurities, Lydia is likely to work long and hard but be a born worrier, especially about finances. She will seldom admit to making mistakes – except perhaps to herself!

Moon in Taurus   This reinforces the stability of the earth sign of Capricorn. Lydia is likely to be sociable, need security, and be loving and sexy. However, she will also be possessive and have a fierce temper. She wouldn't cope well with emotional pressures or too many changes, and would be likely to close her eyes to problems in relationships.

Virgo Ascendant   Yet another earth sign here! Dutiful, methodical, analytical and precise, nothing far from perfect will satisfy Lydia, but what is perfect to her might not be perfect to someone else! She is likely to appear formal, a little aloof, and totally in control. Stability is a necessity for her, and she will try really hard in relationships, often putting her partner's needs before her own. Not openly affectionate, she will be very critical of herself, and of others, and her success or failure will to a large degree depend on the men in her life and how her relationships go.

The above example is a very brief outline, but it shows how to build on the basic information supplied by the Sun placement. It is a worthwhile exercise to try to work out which Moon placement you have in your chart from the descriptions given, so that you can identify the most obvious aspects of your personality. Try to resist consulting the ephemeris until later.

 our Love Lives

PRACTICE

Before we close let's see how much you have learnt so far about the Moon and relationships. All the answers are to be found somewhere this chapter, but they will not be given here. It is up to you to find them, or preferably remember the answers without looking them up!

- What three things have we looked at to see how the Moon placement relates to our overall personality and how we come across and feel inside?

- Is the Moon considered basically masculine or feminine?

- The Moon takes 26 days to pass through the whole zodiac. True or false?

- What does the Moon placement in the chart show us?

- The Moon placement alters each year, so it is necessary to look up your new Moon sign each year. True or false?

- It is said to be easier to stop bleeding during a Full Moon than at any other time. True or false?

CHAPTER 2
MOON PLACEMENTS

We have taken our initial steps on the journey towards self-discovery. We are now going to continue by looking at the Moon placements within each zodiac sign. As we have already stated, the way to work out your own personal Moon sign is given in the Appendix.

We are going to start by looking at the Moon in each of the 12 signs. We will then link this information with all the other Moon placements. Please remember that the information given relates only to Moon sign compatibilities. For a full assessment of compatibility other factors need to be taken into account. However, Moon compatibility provides a very good starting-point.

MOON IN ARIES

Ruler: Mars.
Type: Cardinal fire, masculine/positive.
Famous Moon in Aries people: Marlon Brando, Susan Hampshire, Ingrid Bergman, Alan Alda.

The Moon in the fire sign of Aries gives its owner an enthusiastic nature, the ability for quick thinking (often coming across as not thinking at all) and even quicker reactions, with a tendency towards impatience. This person wants to get things done, and quickly. Likely to be optimistic and take risks, they plan on a large scale but ignore small details. Their feelings are likely to run high, and this is certainly a passionate person, who will experience great highs,

although these may be short-lived, and it is likely that underneath all the exuberance, this person will be insecure, needing constant support and applause from onlookers. Aries Moon people are very emotional types, very romantic and often quite dreamy, and find the best relationships with people who are independent, witty and aloof at first meeting, and with whom they can be friends as well as lovers.

The Aries Moon person likes courtship, loves the game-playing associated with relationships in their early stages, but is likely to lose interest once the spontaneity goes, or if the other person is won over too easily. Much preferring someone who seems out of reach or out of bounds, the Aries Moon person needs someone who will keep them guessing, and be strong, exciting, warm and sexy.

Aries Moons love making plans for dates, and often shower the object of their affection with tokens of their love. Men with this placement will find themselves attracted to women who are strong, probably quite demanding and critical but who are essentially very feminine in appearance. They will quickly cast off any woman who criticises too much, especially someone who complains that they are not being sexually fulfilled. Women with the Aries Moon placement may find themselves attracted to weak men whom they feel they can control, and are likely to be very strong characters, career-minded and often quite masculine.

Aries Moon people need to lead, to be powerful and dominant, and are likely to deplore criticism and advice, and be quite changeable and moody, so that partners don't know what to expect next. This person will do things on a whim, but may change horses midstream. Likewise the tendency for the Aries Moon person to think they know best, and to set down rules and regulations, will contribute to problems in relationships.

The Aries Moon person knows what they want and need, and has the energy to go for it. Their energy levels are likely to be high, and their sexual needs equally important, but they tend to put their own needs before their partner's, leading to tensions developing in relationships. At worst they can be self-centred, quick-tempered and pushy.

ARIES MOON WITH OTHER MOONS

With Aries Moon   A volatile relationship, with lots of rows, lots of fights, all relatively short-lived but which will cause problems. The need for constant stimulation and change, and the inflexibility of both parties, will also mean that a relationship will be strained. It will probably not last long, unless there are other more positive factors in the full chart.

With Taurus Moon   These two work at different speeds, and so the problem is that one will be impatient and the other feel constantly hurried and hassled. Taurus Moons hate change, whilst Aries Moons need change. This is not a good match, although it could work financially.

With Gemini Moon   Both Aries and Gemini Moons are changeable, and the problem here might be that both parties change too much, and not together. Lots in common on a material and physical level, but little in common otherwise. This is a partnership which will sizzle in the bedroom and be boring and difficult out of it.

With Cancer Moon   Cancer Moons can be very moody, especially if they feel slighted, and Aries Moons can be terribly critical. This could cause difficulties. Not a good combination, Aries Moon's changeability and Cancer Moon's need for a secure and happy home life will mean this could be a total non-starter.

With Leo Moon   A fiery combination, with two strong natures meeting head on. Passionate, vital and alive, both will have problems when opinions differ, as neither will back down and will want to dominate, and the Leo Moon is likely to slip onto 'one of those moods' which really annoy the Aries Moon.

With Virgo Moon   Virgo Moons are very precise, analytical, fussy and organised. This will drive the Aries Moon totally mad. Virgo Moon can also be very prudish, and the physical side of the relationship could be problematical.

With Libra Moon   A reasonably good combination, apart from physically, with both parties getting on well, and strengths and weaknesses equally matched. If the Libra Moon can learn to let go a little more when it comes to sex, this could be a great relationship.

With Scorpio Moon   This will be passionate, magnetic and intense, but once the initial thrill has worn off, both parties will

realise that they are total opposites when it comes to what they want from a relationship. Jealousy will be another problem with which to contend if this relationship gets over the initial hurdles.

With Sagittarius Moon A good combination in most ways. Sexually great, emotionally good and likely to be ever changing, this relationship only falters when one side tries to restrain or corner the other.

With Capricorn Moon A difficult combination, because the Capricorn Moon will be too earthy and stubborn, disliking the constant changes the Aries Moon brings. Probably best to steer clear of this combination.

With Aquarius Moon This relationship has every chance of standing the test of time, once the Aquarian Moon has decided they feel able to make a commitment. Sexually compatible, this couple will probably end up being nomads.

With Pisces Moon This combination could work, given time and sufficient patience by both parties, although the effort of it all could mean that the relationship didn't reach first base. Lots of differences here, but romantically a lot of common ground.

MOON IN TAURUS

Ruler: Venus.
Type: Fixed earth, feminine/negative.
Famous Moon in Taurus people: Elton John, Bill Clinton, Carrie Fisher, Julie Walters.

Taurus is an earth sign, and those with the Moon in Taurus (of which I am one) are likely to be very earthy, preferring solidity to anything unstable, changing or fluid. This person needs security, and is emotional and passionate, although this is kept under control for the most part, especially in the initial stages of a relationship.

Taurus Moons don't like rapid change. They need time to prepare for change and accept it. Cautious, sympathetic and reserved, the Taurus Moon is likely to be very stubborn, have fixed opinions and

LOVE SIGNS FOR BEGINNERS

habits, and be rather restrained and materialistic, liking their creature comforts.

This is a practical person who keeps battling on to the end and who has great inner strength. An affectionate person, the Taurus Moon likes, and even demands, physical contact, although they are normally patient and undemanding. Sometimes they have a problem separating love from sex, and sex will always be a vitally important part in a loving relationship. These are strongly sexed people, loving and romantic, although they may find it difficult to express their love in words. They also have terrible tempers when things go wrong.

Love itself will be important to the Taurus Moon, who will also be quite sensual although often unadventurous sexually. Loyal and true, the Taurus Moon is looking for depth and meaning in a relationship. They need a soul-mate on whom they can depend. Not for them the one-night-stand or affair. They need a permanent relationship, and are unlikely to stray once a bond has been formed. They react violently if their partner loses interest, becoming quite possessive at times, although they often totally ignore the root cause of problems in the relationship if it suits their purpose. They cannot function effectively if there are problems on the home front, and may therefore pretend they don't exist. Once an emotional problem is faced, however, they can sink into a very deep depression. A stable home life is vital to their survival, and they will seldom end a relationship unless all possible avenues for happiness have been exhausted.

This person appreciates the good things of life – fabrics which feel nice, fine foods or perfumes, and so on. Ladies who are involved with a Taurus Moon male should make every effort to look great, smell great and cook a great meal. Taurus Moon men will most likely have a strong attachment to their mothers, and will seek a partner who is passive and homely. Problems can arise when they see their partner as either too dependent or too independent.

TAURUS MOON WITH OTHER MOONS

With Aries Moon   Quite a good combination, with earth and fire both represented, but likely to be problematical because both signs

work in different ways. Tensions could run high, leading to arguments, rows and irritations.

With Taurus Moon Two Moons in the same sign means both parties will think along the same lines, sharing the same values and needs, but this could become boring and lack excitement. That aside, it could work well.

With Gemini Moon Gemini Moon people aren't into physical things, preferring mental stimulation and communication. That would be fine, but could cause problems in the bedroom. Other difficulties could lie in the fact that Taurus Moon needs security, which isn't really that important to the Gemini Moon.

With Cancer Moon A great relationship. Everything is set for the perfect couple. Both Taurus and Cancer Moon people need a happy home environment. Trouble could come with Cancer Moon's tendency to sulk, be moody and need the family around all the time, but Taurus Moon could easily cope with that given time.

With Leo Moon A reasonable combination, once both parties have agreed not to be too fixed and obstinate. Both are likely to be loyal and faithful. This combines with the potential for a sexually fulfilling relationship to make for a good match.

With Virgo Moon Two earth Moons don't always make for a good partnership. In many ways this combination will work well, but Virgo Moon makes for a fussy person who will irritate the Taurus Moon and cause friction. Life in the bedroom could become a little staid.

With Libra Moon Another reasonable combination, with both parties getting on well at home, and making a good team. Both signs are ruled by Venus, planet of love and peace, so harmony will be of great importance.

With Scorpio Moon These are opposing Moons, and so there is likely to be an attraction of opposites, deep feelings and mutual bonds. This combination will either be brilliant, passionate and fulfilling, or a total disaster. Although good sexually, problems could occur through jealousy and possessiveness.

With Sagittarius Moon Not a good combination, as there are far too many differences to work through, which would take a lot of patience and time to deal with properly. The Taurus Moon needs security, attention and stability, whereas the Sagittarius Moon needs

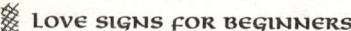 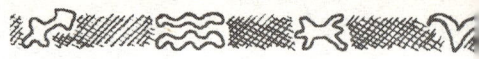

change, freedom and lots of personal space.

With Capricorn Moon Security, stability and comfort matter to both these signs. The problem will come when the Capricorn Moon spends what seems to be too long at work and not enough time at home. Not prone to outward shows of affection, the Capricorn Moon won't give the Taurus Moon enough cuddles and hugs, so problems will arise.

With Aquarius Moon Both signs are very fixed in ideas and opinions, and unfortunately these will differ markedly. This does not make for a good relationship. Squabbles would arise pretty early on in the relationship, neither party would admit they were at fault, and the relationship might not take off at all.

With Pisces Moon A good match this, with both parties being romantic, physical and openly affectionate. Pisces Moons don't need quite as much security as Taurus Moons, and this could cause problems, but both will work well together and have a comfortable and happy home life.

MOON IN GEMINI

Ruler: Mercury.
Type: Mutable air, masculine/positive.
Famous Moon in Gemini people: Joan Baez, Roger Daltry, Brigitte Bardot, Fred Astaire.

Someone with the Moon in Gemini is likely to be very changeable, and those around them are unlikely to understand them fully. Though unpredictable and inconsistent they are also quick to adapt to change.

Because of their need to flit from one thing to another in search of stimulation, the Gemini Moon may have problems with relationships, needing lots of space, lots of freedom and lots of variety to keep them happy. Even though they love to learn and will read a great deal, they often lose interest quickly both in a subject

and in another person. They hate being restricted, committed or tied down. They want a relationship to be fun at all times. As a result, many people with the Moon in this sign remain single for a long time, although they have many friends, being chatty, fairly extrovert, witty and amusing.

There seems to be a permanent problem with thinking about things, and sometimes the Gemini Moon may not think at all, or think too much and lose touch with emotional matters completely. Gemini Moon men are often difficult to understand, and are likely to leave a relationship when problems arise, especially if they concern money or career.

Restless people, Gemini Moons find it impossible to keep secrets, will probably gossip, be flirtatious and impatient, and need to talk about their feelings at great length. If there is a worry, it will be discussed, unless it is a big problem, in which case it will be ignored.

Interested in communication (Gemini is ruled by Mercury – messenger to the gods), the Gemini Moon is likely to have an interest in current affairs and recent inventions, making their home quite a clutter of gadgetry.

A Gemini Moon will be quite magnetic, with ever-changing emotions, feelings and passions, and an intensity which is quite tangible. The need to understand and communicate effectively will be strongly apparent, and if there is a strong bond in the communication field, a reasonably good chance exists for a good relationship all round.

To win over a Gemini Moon it is better to be a friend first, then move on to being something more. Take time over this, however, as the Gemini Moon will hate someone who comes on too strong, too quickly.

This person will sense things, have gut feelings about situations and people, and usually prove to be right in their initial appraisal of a situation. A Gemini Moon makes for a person who likes to know all there is to know about other people, but who may not always be so giving of information about themselves.

Love signs for beginners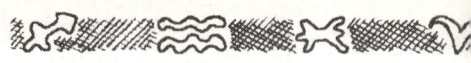

Gemini Moon with Other Moons

With Aries Moon   Not a great combination, and boredom could easily set in. The Aries Moon just will not understand the changeable nature of the Gemini Moon, although it could just work, given that the Gemini Moon will love the fire of the Aries Moon.

With Taurus Moon   A reasonable combination, although problems will arise with the Gemini Moon failing to understand why the Taurus Moon needs security and hates change, and finding it all too much like hard work. The Taurus Moon will be jealous and possessive, as with most earth signs, and this could be a problem, given the flirtatious nature of the Gemini Moon.

With Gemini Moon   Maybe these two are just too much alike for a relationship to succeed. It could work if both parties move in the same direction all the time. The problem is that the relationship could just fall apart because neither party is around long enough for a proper bond to be created.

With Cancer Moon   Cancer Moons are very domesticated, hate change and will infuriate a Gemini Moon. Whilst the home might be comfortable and warm, the Gemini Moon will never understand the Cancer Moon's moods, and so this is a relationship which should perhaps be left alone.

With Leo Moon   Both these people are witty, warm and personable. This is a combination which could work, with lots of excitement, parties, discussions and variety.

With Virgo Moon   Two signs ruled by Mercury means lots of talk, lots of communication but maybe little passion, too much analysing of the other party and too many tensions because of the Virgo Moon's tendency to worry over every little thing.

With Libra Moon   Initial problems could beset this couple, but given time, this is a relationship which really could work well, as each will understand the other. Libra Moons need harmony and peace in their lives, and provided this is given to them, the relationship stands every chance of going the distance.

With Scorpio Moon   Passionate, intense and deep, this is a great relationship, on the assumption that the Gemini Moon wishes to give in return. The problem could be that this won't happen, in which case the Gemini Moon person will just up and leave.

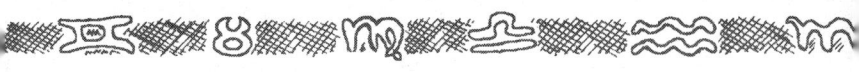

With Sagittarius Moon These are opposing Moons, so there may be a strong attraction. Freedom will matter to both parties, but that could be a problem in a relationship, as both parties will dislike any form of restriction, and could end up going in totally opposite directions.

With Capricorn Moon Another reasonably good combination. The only difficulty may lie in the Gemini Moon's need to be flirtatious, which the Capricorn Moon will not understand at all. Capricorn Moons are possessive and jealous, and lots of rows could ensue. The Gemini Moon might also find the whole thing too routine and lacking in excitement.

With Aquarius Moon This combination could work well, as both signs will have similar ideas. However, the chances are that they will just pass like ships in the night, never bothering too much to find out whether it would have worked or not.

With Pisces Moon If Gemini Moon tried to be a little more romantic and less flirtatious, this relationship could work, as there is a lot of common ground here. Pisces Moons really care, and will work to keep the relationship going. Given the chance, this could be a truly good combination.

PRACTICE

We have now covered the first three Moon signs, looking at the characteristics of each, and at how the Moon signs relate with each other. There is still a long way to go, but before moving on take time to test your newly acquired knowledge.

- Aries Moons are changeable, adaptable and restless. Is this generally true or not?

- Two Aries Moons are likely to get on like a house on fire. True or false?

- Taurus Moons are never judgemental, never possessive and hardly ever jealous. True or false?

- Taurus and Scorpio are opposing signs. True or false?

MOON IN CANCER

Ruler: Moon.
Type: Cardinal water, feminine/negative.
Famous Moon in Cancer people: Giorgio Armani, Janis Joplin, Omar Khayyam, Olivia Newton-John.

As we know, Cancer is ruled by the Moon, and Moon in Cancer makes for a deeply caring, emotional person. This person is exceptionally sensitive, imaginative, caring, domesticated and home-loving, but also likely to be rather moody and over-emotional at times. Likely to have a psychic tendency, or at the very least to be interested in such matters, this person will be very aware of the moods of other people, and needs love almost as much as daily food and drink.

They can often be very manipulative when it comes to matters of the heart. These people like to feel they are in control, and can often take on people with problems because it makes them feel superior. They really do suffer terribly from feelings of inadequacy, and fear separation, divorce and loss of family.

Men especially can be very demanding of home-comforts from their partners, right down to home-cooked meals and a spotless house, and if their needs aren't met, rather than look for another partner, they are likely to go home and tell their mother all about it. Cancer Moons are close to their mothers, and often 'mother' other people, irrespective of gender. They like to have someone to look after and also like to plan for the future.

In love, the Cancer Moon is all or nothing. They are warm and sensitive lovers, to whom sex isn't merely a physical thing but a giving and receiving of love and affection between two people. The object of their affection is likely to be the only thing which matters, and you can often hear Cancer Moon people talking incessantly about their partner, suggesting that without them, there would be no reason to live. Cancer Moons are often terribly possessive and jealous. Their partner can start to feel suffocated and the Cancer Moon will then be terribly hurt.

Criticism of any kind will wound the Cancer Moon, and often they are upset by imagined slights rather than something tangible. They will then be very withdrawn, quiet and unresponsive, sometimes for days at a time. The only way round this is to place food in front of them, as food is not only a source of comfort but a real joy.

Cancer is ruled by the Moon, and so these people will be terribly affected by the Moon's phases, especially Full or New Moons.

As with Sun sign Cancer people, Cancer Moons hate change and disruption. Tradition, family and heritage will matter immensely and making sure there is sufficient money for the future will be a major project throughout most if not all of their working life. They need people around them who share their values and are essentially home-lovers

CANCER MOON WITH OTHER MOONS

With Aries Moon Fire and water don't mix terribly well. Water tends to put out the fire, and this could be the case in this combination, although initial appearances may indicate otherwise. The Aries Moon will be too outspoken and noisy; the Cancer Moon prefers something or someone a little more reserved.

With Taurus Moon Both these signs are very domesticated, home-loving people, and therefore they have a lot in common. Sex may be a little unexciting, but this is a good combination which will most probably stay the course.

With Gemini Moon Cancer Moons can be terribly moody, and the Gemini Moon really won't be able to cope with that. Gemini Moons don't seem to need affection, preferring to think and communicate. That isn't really Cancer Moon's scene. Gemini Moons need space and freedom, and problems could occur there.

With Cancer Moon This could be a fairly good combination, until both parties get into a mood at the same time, when there could be disruptions or, conversely, long periods with little communication. It would be far better to have someone a little less sensitive. The troubles which could crop up around the Full Moon could make front page news!

With Leo Moon This could work well. A combination where there would need to be a little give and take on both sides to make for a truly happy relationship. Both parties are warm and loving and the only problems could occur over financial overspending on the part of the Leo Moon.

With Virgo Moon Another promising combination, although it could fall foul of Virgo Moon's tendency to criticise and Cancer Moon's sensitivity. Virgo Moons love to look after people just as much as the Cancer Moon does. Sexually a little dull perhaps, but otherwise a good match.

With Libra Moon This is a good match. Both parties hate disruption, and harmony would prevail at all costs. Libra Moons are very thoughtful and will probably come over to the Cancer Moon's way of working eventually.

With Scorpio Moon Probably one of the best matches for Cancer Moon. Both parties should understand each other really well. The only problem could come with sexual matters, as the Scorpio Moon may be more highly sexed than the Cancer Moon, and neither sign forgives or forgets a hurt or slight. Even 'I have a headache' will be remembered for ever by the Cancer Moon.

With Sagittarius Moon After the initial attraction has worn off, this couple could find themselves with nothing in common. The Cancer Moon would be far too possessive for the Sagittarius Moon. Both signs are so different in outlook, modes of behaviour and feelings that it probably wouldn't be worth the effort in the first place.

With Capricorn Moon Opposing Moons, with both needing security, loving tradition and needing to look towards financial security. This could work well, unless the Capricorn Moon criticises the other partner or has a demanding job, in which case the Cancer Moon will spend a lot of time alone.

With Aquarius Moon A good chance that this relationship could succeed. The Aquarius Moon may seem a little avant-garde at times, but the Cancer Moon could learn to cope if they felt the risk was worth taking. However, to outsiders this match certainly wouldn't be made in heaven.

With Pisces Moon Two water signs here, with lots of romance, passion and sex. A brilliant combination, possibly the best. Home will be a place in which to relax, talk problems through, be together and be happy. A match made in heaven!

MOON IN LEO

Ruler: Sun.
Type: Fixed fire, masculine/positive.
Famous Moon In Leo People: Margaret Thatcher, Winston Churchill, Zola Budd, Tom Selleck.

This person really knows how to make an entrance or an exit, and also remain centre-stage. They are magnetic personalities who need to feel they have made a mark on the world. Cheerful, proud and impressive, dramatic and intuitive, they can be terribly vain, self-occupied, self-centred or just plain over-the-top. Likely to put the object of their affection on a pedestal which is totally unrealistic, they expect their partner to be well turned out, well dressed and well mannered at all times. This person will not tolerate anybody saying something which, to them, shows them up, even if it is meant in fun, so partners have to learn to know the limits of humour.

These people love to give and also expect to receive – and that applies to everything, from affection through to admiration. Loyal and affectionate, and a grand person in all ways, the Leo Moon person will love to have a good time and will probably have several love affairs, or even marriages, before settling down properly. Men with the Leo Moon are normally attracted to glamorous women, and first impressions definitely go a long way. Leo Moon men go overboard with presents, phone-calls and tokens of affection.

This person also needs to be needed, loved and praised, probably more so than anything else. Criticism will wound them considerably, but they themselves can be terribly bossy and arrogant, a problem which will crop up in any relationship they enter into. Strangely, they can also become terribly depressed and then will really need a shoulder to cry on. Only someone very close will see this side of their characters, as they don't like too many people to see their vulnerability.

This is a stubborn person who is often dissatisfied with life generally, and will seek to improve their lot, no matter what, sometimes acting first and thinking a lot later. Even when they have everything, they are still on the lookout for something a little better. Unlikely to want to change their behaviour any, thinking any problems must have stemmed from the other party, this is a person who is genuinely friendly, warm and open, but underneath rather shy, uncertain and lacking in confidence.

People with Moon in Leo need to have a loving relationship in order to feel totally happy. Faced with a break-up, as they will do all they can to keep things ticking over until another avenue for their affection is found.

Leo Moons are tender, sensual, romantic and affectionate lovers, but expect the same in return. They also expect a partner to be amusing, clever, glamorous and a good listener, and to watch the pennies, as this is something the Leo Moon has a great problem with. Don't expect the Leo Moon to want to stay at home much, as they love going out, and if they are staying in, they expect to be entertaining guests rather than watching TV. They also expect their partner to be on their side 100 per cent and allow them to be centre-stage.

Leo Moon with Other Moons

With Aries Moon   This could be a good combination once both parties got used to the other's need to be noticed. Aries Moons can be terribly blunt, and that could cause problems, but otherwise a good match, with lots of excitement.

With Taurus Moon   A great combination. Both parties mirror each other well, love comfort and need affection and attention. Lots of passion and genuine love for each other here. However, both dislike being told what to do or bossed, and that could cause problems, as both are fairly bossy. There could be lots of arguments and competition.

With Gemini Moon A busy social life would be guaranteed with this partnership. However, it could leave both parties too tired for each other. The Gemini Moon would probably be the first to give up.

With Cancer Moon The Cancer Moon would really love to look after the Leo Moon, and the home would be a haven for both. Problems could come with the Leo Moon's need to be boss, and the Cancer Moon's oversensitivity and moodiness because of their realisation that they are not always in control.

With Leo Moon Fireworks are possible, as both want to be top dog, at home and at work. Initially, the attraction would be great, but the relationship probably wouldn't stay the course.

With Virgo Moon Leo Moons will hate the Virgo Moon's criticism, however well it is disguised. Otherwise a pretty good match, with the Virgo Moon pondering the needs of the Leo Moon. This relationship could work, if given the necessary time and patience.

With Libra Moon Libra Moons will bend over backwards to keep the peace, and this could really be a good combination, especially since both parties appreciate the finer things in life. The only problems could come in the bedroom, as the Libra Moon can be a little prudish.

With Scorpio Moon Maybe too much passion and jealousy here to allow a long-term relationship to develop. It would work well if the Sun signs were compatible. Both signs are very sexy, so physically there would be no problem.

With Sagittarius Moon Lots of fun but not a lot in common could lead this to being a pretty poor match, despite them both being fire signs. The Sagittarian Moon needs more freedom than the Leo Moon would be prepared to give.

With Capricorn Moon The chances are that the Leo Moon would find the Capricorn Moon a little dull and over-practical. Another problem could be that the Capricorn Moon works so hard that they have no time for a social life, which is essential to the Leo Moon. A likelihood of arguments here.

With Aquarius Moon Opposing Moons here, so there is every possibility that there will be an attraction and lots of passionate sex. However, once that dies down, the Aquarius Moon may just be too embarrassing for the Leo Moon to tolerate for long.

With Pisces Moon Romantic, warm and loving, this fire and water relationship is quite good, once both parties learn that the Leo Moon person will always be the boss, and the Leo Moon person has learnt that a silence isn't a sulk.

MOON IN VIRGO

Ruler: Mercury.
Type: Mutable earth, feminine/negative.
Famous Moon in Virgo people: Vanessa Redgrave, Lord Nelson, John F. Kennedy, Gloria Vanderbilt.

Creative, practical and clever, these are totally unromantic, fussy people who are inclined to be overly critical, letting their head govern their heart, thus alienating those around them. Very little room here for shades of grey. Things are always either black or white, wrong or right, and they need to be right at all times.

Methodical, neat and tidy, the Virgo Moon is often emotionally inhibited, seeming aloof, reserved and cold because of their shyness. Ever the realist, these people are, however, very sexual and giving, once they learn that it is acceptable to give free rein to emotions every now and again. They seem to have no problem in sexual relationships, possibly because they separate the emotional side from the physical, although they can be terribly prudish. Men with the Moon in Virgo rarely understand their partners, ending up with problematical relationships through bad choices or through using women for their own motives. They often seem afraid to show their true feelings at all, which creates difficulties for both sexes.

Likely to suffer with their nerves, and to be over-anxious and lack assertiveness, Moon in Virgo none the less has a capacity for hard work, especially detailed work, but switches off easily too.

Moon in Virgo people often become quite obsessive about their health, and can exclude everyone else for the sake of their fitness regime. Also interested in food and hygiene, these people are good cooks, although they are fussy eaters, and will worry endlessly about most things, including the state of their own health and thus can become very introspective and self-doubting. This can cause extreme problems in relationships, as can the fact that these people are obsessively tidy and will clean up after someone whilst they are still using the object concerned! They will also hate a noisy household. These people need quiet. They also need to feel useful.

Virgo Moons have lots of problems with relationships because they are over-analytical about the other party, their motives, whether they are right for them or not, and so on. This often greatly diminishes the warm glow of the loving relationship.

VIRGO MOON WITH OTHER MOONS

With Aries Moon A reasonably good combination, as the Aries Moon will keep the relationship exciting. However, this could cause problems for the Virgo Moon, who would find the whole thing too fast-moving, noisy and impractical.

With Taurus Moon Two earth signs which relate well together, although there may be a little staleness at times. Both signs expect and like the same things where home and family are concerned, but there won't be much romance.

With Gemini Moon Both signs are ruled by Mercury, so talking shouldn't be a problem. The Virgo Moon could have problems with the Gemini Moon's tendency towards infidelity, but it won't be a boring relationship.

With Cancer Moon These two could just rub each other up the wrong way after an initially promising start. The Cancer Moon just won't be able to stand the critical ways of the Virgo Moon, although both will understand each other's moods and share sensitivities.

With Leo Moon A reasonable chance of success with this relationship, although the Leo Moon will definitely rule the roost. There might be too many parties, too much noise and activity for the Virgo Moon, but life will certainly be lived to the full.

With Virgo Moon Far too much going against this relationship for it to work well, if at all. Initially, they will understand each other well, but lots of problems will have to be worked through.

With Libra Moon   Peace, harmony and comfort will abound in this relationship. A good combination, once the Virgo Moon adapts to the fact that the Libra Moon likes to socialise in all the best places, which cost pounds not pennies!

With Scorpio Moon   A lot of intensity and passion from the Scorpio Moon could cause problems for the introspective Virgo Moon. This relationship could work, or fail abysmally. A lot depends on the Sun sign placements.

With Sagittarius Moon   A difficult combination, but one which could work well, with both sides learning from the other and fun being had by both. If time were given to this relationship, it could be a good match, although perhaps it would take too much time!

With Capricorn Moon   Both earth signs, these two are likely to work well, if a little unadventurously. Both signs tend to be hard-working, and so there may be little time spent at home together.

With Aquarius Moon   These two wouldn't understand each other at all. Possibly this relationship might not move off first base. Aquarian Moons love to shock and be different, and this is something that the Virgo Moon couldn't stomach at any cost.

With Pisces Moon   Opposing Moons, which can attract once both parties learn to adapt. This could be a really cosy couple, with both parties learning and helping each other along, creating a great home environment, especially for children.

PRACTICE

We have now covered a further three Moon signs, and looked at how these interrelate. Again, it is time to test your knowledge.

- Leo Moons are normally quite reserved, hating parties and preferring to spend time at home. True or false?

- Cancer and Capricorn are opposite signs. True or false?

- Leo and Gemini Moons work really well together, because both are fire signs, ruled by Mars. True or false?

- Virgo Moons are very interested in health and fitness. As a result, they relate very well with Aquarian Moons. True or false?

MOON IN LIBRA

Ruler: Venus.
Type: Cardinal air, masculine/positive.
Famous Moon in Libra people:
Michael Caine, Dyan Cannon, Billy Jean King, Bernard Levin.

Ever the diplomat, hating upsets and scenes, the Libra Moon person will be well-mannered to the nth degree, often appearing shallow and fickle, yet really meaning well, and being good company.

It is essential to the Libra Moon that their homelife be a haven of peace and tranquillity. Tending to idealise love and being terribly romantic, very old-fashioned and somewhat prudish, these people expect the object of their affection to have no past, no previous lovers and no skeletons in the cupboard. It is also essential that the Libra Moon has a relationship all the time, as they do not take well to living and being alone. If there is no current romantic interest, it is likely that the Libra Moon will pour all their attention into their family. They often fail to see the reality of a relationship, preferring to concentrate on the paperback-novel type of romance, which rarely seems to come around. This tendency often means that the Libra Moon will stay in a relationship which isn't working because they hate the thought of going it alone.

Men with the Moon in Libra can be difficult lovers, as they often have little respect for women, seeing them as decorative accessories and expecting their partner to look brilliant but say very little. These men often gravitate towards women who have little or no ambition of their own. In the case of both sexes, Libra Moon people will, themselves, always look very well turned out, if not immaculate, and be polite, well mannered and courteous. As with Libra Sun types, those with a Libra Moon will be indecisive, and often need a prod to get them moving.

Charming and idealistic, some would say quixotic, these people are not above manipulating others for their own ends, and can be hypercritical. Forever the optimist, these are determined people, and will get what they want most of the time, standing their corner in even the toughest of situations.

Just as love is everything to the Cancer Moon, romance is of paramount importance to the Libra Moon. Security will also matter, and once in a stable relationship, the Libra Moon will be very loving and romantic, even if at times there will be elements of emotional insecurity.

Libra Moons tend to be very influenced by what their partner wants and expects. Attractive and yet often fickle, these people want the perfect partner, someone who looks good, is quiet, polite, uncritical and creative. Once they find this person, they will do everything in their power to make it a perfect relationship.

Libra Moon with Other Moons

With Aries Moon   Initially promising, but the Aries Moon will be too fast-moving, brash and impatient for the Libra Moon. This relationship is likely to wither away due to conflicting interests.

With Taurus Moon   Both signs are ruled by Venus, so there's a lot of love and attraction here. Could work well, once the sexual hurdle is overcome. Taurus Moons are far more physical and sexual than Libra Moons.

With Gemini Moon   Gemini Moons can be very flirtatious, but Libra Moons can be equally fickle. This combination may work, given time, or just fall apart.

With Cancer Moon   Both home-loving and peaceable signs, so this would work well. Cancer Moon's moodiness would irritate the Libra Moon at times, but this could be overcome with a little understanding.

With Leo Moon   Both signs are romantic, loving and warm, and this could work well, provided the Leo Moon remained boss. Probably one of the better combinations for the Libra Moon.

With Virgo Moon   Not a good match. Too many differences, and

Virgo Moon's critical and analytical ways would cause a lot of problems here. Maybe the fires would go out after a short time.

With Libra Moon   Two like-minded people, both sharing the same values and goals. However, the indecision involved would be problematical if something needed tackling straight away, and perhaps a better combination would be away from the mirror-image.

With Scorpio Moon   Sexy Scorpio Moon might be just a little too intense and passionate for the reserved Libra Moon. Likewise the Libra Moon might appear too shallow to the Scorpio Moon.

With Sagittarius Moon   Sagittarius Moons don't like being organised or restricted. There may be more problems than it's worth here. The whole thing could prove rather a strain.

With Capricorn Moon   This could work once both sides got used to the differences in make-up. Capricorn's coolness and need to attend to business before pleasure would be a major stumbling block.

With Aquarius Moon   A good friendship could blossom into something more. The problem is convincing the Aquarius Moon that they really wanted a relationship in the first place.

With Pisces Moon   Both romantic and loving, this is a relationship which could work well, despite the differing elements involved. Both would help each other and learn from the experience.

MOON IN SCORPIO

Rulers: Pluto and Mars.
Type: Fixed water, feminine/negative.
Famous Moon in Scorpio people: Alfred Hitchcock, Bram Stoker, Elizabeth Taylor, Dame Margaret Rutherford.

Moon in Scorpio is a good placement, since the Moon's own sign, Cancer, is also a feminine and negative water sign. Emotional, deep, secretive, very sensitive, often moody (much the same as the Cancer

Moon), the Scorpio Moon is also very magnetic, energetic, active, possessive and private. This is an acutely intense person who can shift from altruism to selfishness in seconds. Sometimes they give everything they possess emotionally for other people, and sometimes they give nothing and harbour deep grudges. This is a person of extremes.

Scorpio Moon people will go all out for what they want, and that includes the object of their affection. They can manipulate people and situations to engineer their desired response. Often coming across as overly strong, the Scorpio Moon person will sometimes rehearse a conversation in advance, to make sure that it goes as they intend. These people also need a fulfilling sexual relationship, although they are also very romantic. Physical things will matter a lot to the Scorpio Moon (some would say they are just preoccupied by sex) and they will also be interested in things mystic or mysterious, being exceptionally intuitive.

Often problems occur for them because they come across as uncaring at times when a caring approach is needed. This is probably part and parcel of their need to keep something of themselves secret from the rest of the world, for fear of being discovered, or even hurt. Conversely, there are other Scorpio Moon people who are very openly emotional, which just goes to show their complexity. These people are often just difficult to fathom, even to those close to them. They are jealous and possessive with partners, and may even resent their partners' former relationships. They need to feel loved in a big way, but won't want someone who pries into all the corners of their life, as they need some space where nobody goes. Unfortunately they don't appreciate that others may feel likewise. Really quite sensitive underneath it all, their vulnerability is often well hidden under the mask of the capable, hard-working person.

Men with the Moon in Scorpio are often very close to their mothers (like the Cancer person), and whilst they will gravitate towards strong women who mirror their mother, they may resent their partner as a result, never forgetting those who hurt them or who they feel have done them wrong. In fact neither sex ever forgets anything.

They will remember conversations, places or dates long after others have forgotten. They also have a knack of knowing exactly what the other person is thinking, and if they feel that they aren't being told something, they will just up and ask.

Needing control in a relationship, these are stubborn people who both need and expect to be admired, loved and applauded. The Scorpio Moon is passionate, tactile and often obsessive. They are very loving to those whom they respect and care for, and they never forget a favour done. They dislike being in debt and will likewise never forget anything owed to them.

Scorpio Moons need a partner who is also a friend. They need someone understanding, supportive, passionate, strong yet not domineering, and who will fulfil all their longings and needs. Their apparent cynicism about love may mask a fear of getting hurt. They are romantic, loving and warm people, though very changeable.

SCORPIO MOON WITH OTHER MOONS

With Aries Moon   Both signs have Mars in common, and this could be a very fiery and passionate liaison, but jealousies would soon crop up, as the Aries Moon needs more space than the Scorpio Moon would be willing, or able, to give.

With Taurus Moon   This has a lot going for it, but it may or may not work. Both signs are very tactile and passionate. On the other hand both tend towards jealousy and an inability to forgive.

With Gemini Moon   Jealousies could run high if the Gemini Moon decided to be flirtatious. Too many doubts would ruin the chance of a long-term relationship.

With Cancer Moon   Both signs are very similar in a lot of respects. Romantically this would be a good combination, but there are a lot of problems to deal with before this relationship reaches double figures.

With Leo Moon   A pretty dramatic time would be guaranteed here, and the relationship would definitely have a lot of sparkle (or sparks). Sexually this could be an earth-shattering combination, but the needs and goals of each would be different.

With Virgo Moon   Lots in common here to make for a good relationship all round. The Virgo Moon would do everything possible to make the relationship work, but would the Scorpio Moon resent this?

With Libra Moon   Libra Moon could be a little too prudish for the sexy Scorpio Moon. Both signs work in different ways, want different things and think differently, but the home would at least be peaceful.

With Scorpio Moon   Wow! What a combination. Could burn itself out quickly, with lots of fights and moods, but what a way to go! This could be a great combination, as both would understand each other intimately.

With Sagittarius Moon   Great friends, but perhaps not soul-mates. A lot of fun for both parties, but as relationships go, this is not one of the best. Physically, it would be a poor match.

With Capricorn Moon   Maybe a little more emotional depth and less materialism from the Capricorn Moon would make this a better combination. It could work with a little bending from both sides.

With Aquarius Moon   The Aquarius Moon is very adventurous and unconventional, and this wouldn't sit well with the Scorpio Moon. This is probably one of the worst combinations imaginable.

With Pisces Moon   A good combination. Both loving, sexy, tactile and romantic. Two water signs who would work well together, understand each other, and make a good team.

MOON IN SAGITTARIUS

Ruler: Jupiter.
Type: Mutable fire, masculine/positive.
Famous Moon in Sagittarius people: Glenda Jackson, Charles Bronson, Alice Cooper, Ludwig van Beethoven.

Happy-go-lucky, cheerful, optimistic and restless, the Sagittarian Moon person is sincere and well-meaning, but can be very offhand on occasion, easily upsetting others, not least by their high standards, which must be met at all costs, and by their need to tell people what to do and how to do it. Sometimes they should look at themselves a little more earnestly, and realise that they too dislike being told what to do.

Likely to be intuitive, if not psychic, these people need freedom in relationships, and often travel widely, so that many fail to find a permanent partner. Quite nomadic, needing their own space a lot of the time, they won't be pinned down and don't find commitment easy.

Emotionally, Sagittarian Moons often appear cut off from the rest of society. This is probably because they find great difficulty giving love to other people for fear that it will bind them to those people for ever and thus curtail their personal freedom. Men with the Moon in Sagittarius won't really understand women, or make much effort to do so. As a result, these people are forever bachelor types, even when in a relationship. They need to feel independent and keep their own identity at all costs. They need freedom to pursue their own goals.

Likely to make many mistakes en route to success, both in career and personal matters, these are energetic people, open, honest (if not tactless and insensitive at times), who drift from place to place, situation to situation, with ease, often lacking objectivity. They need their partner to be a good friend, someone whose ego isn't easily bruised, someone who isn't sensitive, is able to stand the knocks and bumps of what is likely to be a difficult relationship, and who won't mind moving around a lot. Their perfect partner is someone who never suffers from jealousy or possessiveness and who is loving, faithful, loyal and sexy, Unfortunately, many people have problems with this, and whilst the honesty and humour of the Sagittarian Moon can be very appealing, it can also be very exasperating. Likely to be the life and soul of the party (even sometimes outshining the Leo counterpart) these are fun people to be around.

If the Sagittarian Moon could get a little nearer to understanding emotions, both their own and other people's, the whole question of relationships would be a lot easier. Sometimes they seem far too attached to moral values taught by their parents.

SAGITTARIUS MOON WITH OTHER MOONS

With Aries Moon   Two fire signs who could pull together or pull apart. Life would certainly be exciting, and there would be a lot of attraction, but maybe this relationship wouldn't go full term.

With Taurus Moon   Taurus Moon people need security and commitment, and can be very jealous and possessive, so this may not be the relationship for the Sagittarius Moon to entertain for too long.

With Gemini Moon   Opposite Moons which could attract or repel. Both signs need space and freedom, so this could work well. Lots of talking, lots of fun but maybe not much chance of reaching first base.

With Cancer Moon   Maybe a lot in common, but also a lot of differences, so this could be a difficult combination. Both parties need something that the other couldn't or wouldn't provide, and the Sagittarian would probably up and leave before long.

With Leo Moon   Leo Moons can be very bossy and domineering, and this wouldn't sit well with the Sagittarius Moon. Lots of social life but little else to offer, once the initial passions had subsided.

With Virgo Moon   Too many restrictions would be placed on the Sagittarian Moon for this to work well. There might be a lot of common ground, but for the relationship to work well long-term, a lot of sacrifices would have to be made by both parties.

With Libra Moon   Libra Moon will work really hard in order for the relationship to flourish, and it may well be worth all the effort, although the whole thing might be a little too inflexible and old-fashioned for the Sagittarius Moon.

With Scorpio Moon   Too many jealousies from the Scorpio Moon for this to work well, if at all. The Sagittarian would feel trapped and the Scorpio Moon's need for occasional privacy would cause no end of problems.

With Sagittarius Moon   Far too many similarities for either party to learn about the inner needs of the other, and the problems with money would be endless. This is a relationship which would have an explosive start but be relatively short-lived.

With Capricorn Moon   Capricorn Moon people need security. That won't mix at all well with the Sagittarius Moon's need for freedom. However, because of the many opposites here, this could work, as the Capricorn's strengths would be the Sagittarian's weaknesses.

With Aquarius Moon   Very unconventional and quite bizarre, this would be some relationship! Lots of excitement, lots of movement and change. Both parties need personal freedom and would easily understand the other's needs.

With Pisces Moon   Romantic and passionate, this relationship stands a good chance of success, as both signs would find something strong and bonding within the relationship.

PRACTICE

Now pause for a while and see how many questions you can answer without looking back.

- Scorpio Moons are passionate, intense and loving in much the same way as Cancer Moons. Both are water signs and both are pre-occupied with sexual matters. Is this statement generally true or false?

- Libra Moons dislike harmonious atmospheres, preferring the challenge of upheaval. True or false?

- Which of the three signs we have just discussed has Jupiter as a ruling planet?

- Because the Moon relates to Cancer, which is a water sign, Libra, which is also governed by the Moon, will be similar in many respects. True or false?

- The planet Venus governs Scorpio. True or false?

- Libra Moon people are governed by the planet Jupiter. True or false?

MOON IN CAPRICORN

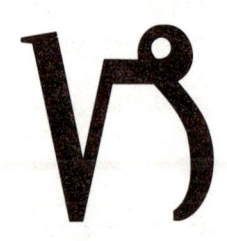

Ruler: Saturn.
Type: Cardinal earth, feminine/negative.
Famous Moon in Capricorn people: Jane Russell, Annie Lennox, Abraham Lincoln, George Washington.

Capricorn Moons are practical, cautious and reserved, and need to feel respected. They are responsible members of the community, often fearing a show of emotion in case it shows up a weak spot in their character. Their tendency towards pessimism often creates problems for them, as does their suspicious nature and tendency to distance themselves from other people. You can normally spot the Capricorn Moon person. They will be in the group but apart from it, observing from the sidelines before taking the plunge and joining in. However, they can be witty and amusing, and able to laugh at themselves, although they hate being laughed at.

Although down to earth, Capricorn Moons are often very idealistic, but hide this side of themselves well. They deal with things as and when they occur, but will worry greatly about the impact this has on other people. Although needing affection deeply, men with the Moon in Capricorn often fear showing affection at all, and will choose someone who is equally reserved, although both sexes really do need emotional security. Likely to have difficulty forming strong emotional bonds, Capricorn Moons throw themselves into work, into anything practical to balance out their lives. They are often well-organised successful people who appear cold, aloof, overly cautious, unapproachable and unfathomable.

Often aware from an early age that life isn't a bed of roses, the person with the Moon in Capricorn will be very independent, shy and withdrawn. Perhaps fearing the loss of control if they become too dependent on another, these people need to feel respected, loved and admired by their partner. They also need to feel trusted.

Not prone to romanticism, these people can be very inhibited, especially about sex or physical pleasures. Not for them cuddles by the fire. Viewing relationships with serious intent, flirtations are not their scene, neither are one-night stands, and rejections will wound them more deeply than outsiders would ever understand. Those with the Moon in Capricorn will often convince themselves that they do not deserve to find a happy relationship, and this may put the dampers on it before it even starts.

The Moon in Capricorn person really needs someone who will make them laugh, be trusting and sincere, quiet yet lively, tidy and punctual to show them that things really can go well, if you have faith and trust. They also need loyal support, emotional and material security, and understanding. Unfortunately they often gravitate towards partners who can offer material security but not the love and affection they need as well.

CAPRICORN MOON WITH OTHER MOONS

With Aries Moon Aries Moon people are too extrovert and noisy for the quiet Capricorn to stand for long. These are people who work at totally opposite ends of the spectrum, so there is little chance of a lasting romance.

With Taurus Moon Two earth signs who get on well. They would be financially secure, and life would run smoothly, but it could be rather dull and uneventful. However, the cuddles might make it all worthwhile.

With Gemini Moon Gemini Moon tends to flirt, and this wouldn't go down at all well with the Capricorn Moon. Neither party would really understand the other's needs sufficiently for this relationship to succeed.

With Cancer Moon Opposite Moons, which could work well or very badly, with an initial attraction and lots of depth. For this to work, the Capricorn Moon would have to curb their criticism and be prepared to put their partner before their career sometimes.

With Leo Moon There would be power struggles here, as both signs like to be in control. Lots of socialising, lots or warmth, but little chance of long-term success.

With Virgo Moon Practical, earthy and solid, but maybe lacking in any depth. This is one of those relationships which may work or may not.

With Libra Moon Probably little romance, and there could be difficulties with conflicting attitudes. This partnership could work well, but it wouldn't always be easy.

With Scorpio Moon Passionate, intense and magnetic, the Scorpio Moon would soon frighten the Capricorn Moon, unless an effort were made to get to grips with feelings and emotions – not an easy task for the Capricorn Moon.

With Sagittarius Moon Fun, love and laughter, but no security at all for the Capricorn Moon. Probably best avoided unless the Sun signs are exceptionally well matched.

With Capricorn Moon Two like-minded pessimistic people, who will need the same things, work towards the same ends, but probably never be at home together due to work commitments. Possibly a good thing!

With Aquarius Moon Unconventional and bizarre, this relationship may be a little too scatty for the Capricorn Moon to stay the course. It would work well if they only saw each other once in a blue moon.

With Pisces Moon Romantic and loving, this relationship will probably frighten the Capricorn Moon, but be a worthwhile experience in the passion stakes. Again it would be necessary for the Capricorn Moon to try to make an effort emotionally.

Moon in Aquarius

Rulers: Saturn and Uranus.
Type: Fixed air, masculine/positive.
Famous Moon in Aquarius people: Melanie Griffith, Muhammed Ali, Claire Bloom, Sir Arthur Conan Doyle.

A brilliant communicator, needing someone who can communicate equally effectively, the Moon in Aquarius person truly needs someone who is on their wavelength, and who will be a friend, first and foremost, before anything else.

Sometimes withdrawn and unpredictable, sometimes sociable, this is a person who can be very erratic, yet imaginative, and charitable. Not for them any tactile behaviour: they are more interested in the mind and communication, often not bothering at all with the emotional side of things.

Independent and likely to hate rules and restrictions, the Moon in Aquarius person is avant garde, broad-minded, determined, active and modern. Men with the Moon in Aquarius may deliberately hide from close relationships because they fear showing a softer side to their personality. Likewise they are often drawn to women who are equally independent, and can often appear totally devoid of any real feelings, preferring to concentrate their energies on group activities rather than on anything one-to-one. Aquarius Moons are friendly with many people but close to few, and even their families will say that they don't really understand them.

They are likely to be loyal and faithful, and respect for their partner is a priority. They need someone who will support them but not be too demanding or clingy. They have a real fear of being restricted by other people. Whilst they will quickly help other people, being naturally friendly and humanitarian, they often fail to admit to problems, leading close friends and family to think they can survive without any help at all.

Eccentric at times, often downright bizarre, unpredictable, intuitive, unconventional and way-out, the Aquarian Moon will love to shock. This is a great way of showing their sense of humour, which they have in abundance. However, they will fail to see that other people might be alarmed, if not taken aback, by some of their antics. This person knows what they want from a partner, but they scare people off by being too detached and cool. It is important to most other signs to know that they are cared for and loved, and the Aquarius Moon must learn to communicate their emotions more to be truly successful in relationships.

AQUARIUS MOON WITH OTHER MOONS

With Aries Moon Lots of verbal banter and lots of excitement, but perhaps too much fire here for the Aquarian Moon to feel comfortable. It could all burn out too quickly.

With Taurus Moon A reasonably good combination, given that both parties are very different. Lots of love and affection, but the Taurus Moon can be possessive at times and that would cause major problems.

With Gemini Moon Two air signs, lots of talk but perhaps too little emotionally and physically here, and little compatibility once the initial impact had worn off.

With Cancer Moon This combination could work given time. The Cancer Moon might find it a strain, however, as they are more possessive than the Aquarius Moon and might need more intimacy and sharing than the Aquarius Moon would be able to give. Likewise the Aquarian Moon might require more personal space.

With Leo Moon Opposite Moons with a lot of attraction, warmth and excitement. This doesn't necessarily mean that the relationship will work, and it could be one which lights up like a sparkler but goes out like a damp squib.

With Virgo Moon An Aquarius Moon wouldn't like the fussy, nit-picking ways of the Virgo Moon. Not a lot of emotion from either side, but a reasonable relationship if neither party wants passion.

With Libra Moon A great combination if the Aquarius Moon tries to make it work. Both parties could work well together to create harmony and happiness, but the Aquarius would have to conform a little.

With Scorpio Moon Passionate and intense, the Scorpio Moon would be too much for the Aquarius Moon to risk. This is one of the worst combinations imaginable. Far too many difficulties.

With Sagittarius Moon Both friendly and open, both needing freedom and independence, this could work well. Lots of excitement, lots of sparkle, and a friendship if nothing else.

With Capricorn Moon The sharing of the Saturn link will create many similarities, but maybe the Capricorn Moon will be too down to earth for the Aquarius Moon. At least the Aquarius Moon would keep their independence, because the Capricorn Moon would probably be working anyway!

With Aquarius Moon   Like-minded, both valuing space and freedom, it would be quite something if they met up in the first place, let alone had a relationship! No passion, no romance and no future really.

With Pisces Moon   Romantic, warm and loving, the Pisces Moon could be a perfect partner, but perhaps the Pisces Moon would find the whole thing too unconventional, while the Aquarius Moon would find it all a little slushy.

MOON IN PISCES

Ruler: Neptune.
Type: Mutable water, feminine/negative.
Famous Moon in Pisces people: Elvis Presley, Robert de Niro, Mata Hari, Cilla Black.

Pisces Moon are intuitive if not psychic, impressionable, friendly, warm, tactile and restless. Sex without love will not be something they entertain readily, although they certainly are highly sexed, both needing and expecting a lot of physical intimacy from their partner. Likely to be very receptive to the feelings of others, leading to confusion as to their own feelings at times, this is a person who readily day-dreams, often exaggerates and becomes fanciful, but can understand others far more easily than they sometimes understand themselves. This is also a person who can become terribly depressed when things go wrong, often turning to outside stimuli at such times in order to cope. They find harsh reality difficult to face, and may resort to alcohol, drugs or an affair.

Men with the Moon in Pisces are often quite chauvinistic, thinking of women as somewhat lesser beings. This causes a lot of problems for relationships even though there is a lot of gentleness and caring involved.

LOVE SIGNS FOR BEGINNERS

Romantic and loving, quiet and thoughtful, the person with the Moon in Pisces is highly impractical, often in love with the idea of love, long before the love actually develops into a proper relationship. Tending to think of relationships as really being like the paperback novels, this is the escapist whose relationship must encompass everything – mental, physical, spiritual, emotional and friendship. Even when in an existing relationship, should something come along which appears to fulfil the requirements, the Moon in Pisces person will just dive headlong in there, often forgetting about their partner at home.

Often enjoying their own company, the Moon in Pisces is very loving and loyal, romantic and giving, and can be guaranteed to help friends out when the going gets tough. However, they often have problems standing their own ground when things get tough for them, needing at that time a partner who is strong and supportive and who will give them the added courage to tackle the problem.

This is a sensitive person, easily upset, who will genuinely care about others, but often fear being rejected if they show too much support. Quite spiritual, this person genuinely needs to give to others, but can often then moan at length about feeling put upon and drained by the demands of other people. There are times when this person just ought to be harder. By the same token, it is unfortunately the case that the Moon in Pisces often falls for someone who needs them rather than someone who is there in support.

For a relationship to succeed with this sign, the partner must be warm and loving, but have a realism to balance out the day-dreaming of the Pisces Moon, financial security, practical nature and above all a sunny disposition.

PISCES MOON WITH OTHER MOONS

With Aries Moon   This is one of those relationships which has a lot of sparkle but may not stay the course. The whole thing might be a touch difficult for both parties.

With Taurus Moon   Both these signs are loving, warm and tactile, and this is a good combination. Security matters to both, and the only problems could come in the bedroom, because each sign expects different things from love-making.

With Gemini Moon Lots of attraction, a lot of communication but maybe too many changes in mood for the Pisces Moon to understand fully. The Gemini person might decide not to stay around long anyway.

With Cancer Moon Both water signs with similar ideals and needs, making for a strong bond. This is probably an ideal match, with everything working well, especially at home.

With Leo Moon Leo Moon will give everything to the object of his or her affection, and this is another relationship, despite opposite elements, which could work well. Supportive and caring, the Leo Moon will be the shoulder for the Pisces Moon at times of crisis.

With Virgo Moon Opposite Moons, which again will either attract or repel. Virgo Moon's tendency to worry, fuss, analyse and nit-pick may cause problems, but nothing that couldn't be overcome with some effort.

With Libra Moon Romantic and loving, another relationship which may work fairly well, although the Pisces Moon may never fully understand the Libra Moon, and there may be times when the sparks don't exist at all, let alone fly.

With Scorpio Moon Both passionate and sexy, this could be some combination. Intense and loving, the Scorpio may think about sex far more than the Pisces, but there is an understanding there which will make the relationship work very well.

With Sagittarius Moon Lots of fun and happiness here, but perhaps a bit of insecurity too, because Sagittarius can be very insensitive, upsetting the Pisces Moon with ease.

With Capricorn Moon This relationship could work well. The Capricorn will provide all the security and stability needed, but the whole thing might lack sparkle, and the Capricorn Moon might spend too much time away from home working late.

With Aquarius Moon A reasonably good relationship, but perhaps not enough romance and too much unpredictability for the Pisces. Both signs can be very idealistic and day-dreamy, so maybe nobody would notice if things weren't working out very well.

With Pisces Moon Tons of romance, love, warmth and understanding. Not a lot of practicalities though, and no end of problems for both parties when things start to get tough.

We have now covered the major part of our journey towards learning more about ourselves and others by means of the Moon placement in our charts. But remember, we can never know everything there is to know about ourselves or about others. Just think what a dull and boring world it would be if we all understood each other from the outset, but how much easier it will be when we learn more about ourselves from our Moon and Sun signs.

Before we move on to look at the Sun or star signs and how they relate to what we have learnt already, it is time to see how much you have assimilated. This time the answers could be found anywhere in the chapter.

PRACTICE

- Brian is a Cancer Moon. Carol is a Pisces Moon. Do you think they stand a good chance of getting on together in a romantic relationship?
- Give four examples of opposing Moons. How would they generally get on?
- How would you think two Leo Moons would get on together?
- Aquarius Moons are very conventional and traditional. True or false?
- Is the Moon considered yin or yang, active or passive?
- Which sign has Neptune as its planet?

MOON AND SUN SIGNS

In this chapter we are going to link Sun signs, or star signs, with the Moon signs already discussed, to look at the individual person, rather than at compatibilities. Once we know more about ourselves, and others, we will have a better chance of determining for ourselves whether or not we are likely to relate well.

Remembering what we learnt during the early stages of our journey, the zodiac sign under which you are born will not change, and most people will know their zodiac sign without having to look it up . Should you feel unsure about which sign you belong to, the dates for each sign will be listed at the start of each section.

You will also remember that the Sun placement in your chart is the essential you – not what you are emotionally (the Moon placement) or how you may appear to outsiders (the rising sign) but how you really are. Career, health and future progression are all to a greater degree linked to the Sun placement in your chart.

Your Sun or star sign is the masculine side of you, your conscious, core personality. As we have also now learnt, the Moon placement in your chart refers to your inner, emotional, feeling characteristics, your feminine, intuitive side.

The aim of this section is to try to link the two together, to discover more about individual characteristics. In some cases it is as if there is a permanent struggle going on between what we think we should do, and what we emotionally want to do. However, it is better to say that the emotional side of you will be modified by the conscious part of you, as more often than not the two placements work fairly harmoniously.

Before we continue, it is worth remembering that women are generally softer in approach than their male counterparts. That doesn't always hold true, but it is worth bearing in mind when looking at characteristics.

MOON IN ARIES

Sun in Aries (21 Mar. – 20 Apr.) Impatient, quick-thinking, enthusiastic and extrovert, but possibly quite self-centred. Romantic, expecting their partner to be the main and only love, this person loves flattery, and will be independent irrespective of gender, but very temperamental.

Sun in Taurus (21 Apr. – 21 May) Ambitious, headstrong, determined, fixed and stubborn, this is an outspoken person who is probably quite artistic. Quick to forgive, quick to explode, but very loving, both sexes will be quite aggressive but adventurous. This is someone who may be both confusing and confused due to the Moon and Sun placements being very different.

Sun in Gemini (22 May – 21 June) Witty, intelligent and a great friend, this is someone who can be very fickle and bitchy at times, but fun to be around all the same. Changeable, and likely to come and go on a whim, they may be a terrible flirt and dislike being tied down to anything or anybody.

Sun in Cancer (22 June – 23 July) Understanding of others and likely to be good in business, this person will be quite a go-getter, jealous, sensitive and emotional, faithful and loyal, and will have problems relating this softer, sensitive side of themselves to the brashness of their Sun placement. As a result, there will be more mood swings than normal! Family will matter a lot, but so will career.

Sun in Leo (24 July – 23 Aug.) Two fire placements, which join to create an imposing person, who will be very self-centred, fast-moving, hot-headed, bossy and determined, but a wonderfully passionate and exciting lover. The down side is a temperamental nature linked with an occasionally inconsiderate attitude.

Sun in Virgo (24 Aug. – 23 Sept.) Quick-thinking but equally quick to scold, this person is normally capable of doing many jobs at the same time, will stop at nothing to get what they want, and will be quite unemotional by comparison with other Aries Moons. Loyal and supportive but needing constant reassurance, this person will be sensitive to criticism and reluctant to change.

Sun in Libra (24 Sept. – 23 Oct.)   Intuitive and clever but a touch too impatient, and likely to start things and not see them through, this is someone who is likely to have quite an explosive temper, and find it very difficult to deal with problems. This person needs lots of hugs but will be very independent. The Libra Sun helps to soften the impact of the Aries Moon, but this person may never find a relationship which is totally satisfactory, as they tend to change horses midstream too often.

Sun in Scorpio (24 Oct. – 22 Nov.)   What a combination – intensity, fire, jealousy, determination and passion. This person has a quick fuse, but is a strong character and an exciting lover. Men with this combination can be very egotistical and chauvinistic, whereas women are likely to be very masculine in attitude and somewhat overbearing.

Sun in Sagittarius (23 Nov. – 21 Dec.)   The gambler and risk-taker of the group. This is the person who will have an 'easy come, easy go' attitude, despite a fairly bad temper when things don't go their way, and be always on the move, in fact quite hyperactive, making permanent relationships difficult. Once in a relationship, however, this person sticks like glue.

Sun in Capricorn (22 Dec. – 20 Jan.)   Ambitious and determined to get there no matter what or who stands in the way, this is a stubborn person, who will expect much from their partner. Though friendly, humorous and practical, this person is quite a power-house of passion underneath it all.

Sun in Aquarius (21 Jan. – 19 Feb.)   Though fun-loving and outgoing, this is someone who can be very judgmental, unpredictable and unemotional, and as such they may be a difficult person to get along with. Likely to hate routine and have a terrible temper, this is someone who strives to retain their own independence within a relationship.

Sun in Pisces (20 Feb. – 20 Mar.)   Great friend, lots of fun to be with, a hard worker, but a problem where relationships are concerned, because they are just too sensitive by half, although there will be a lot of romantic yearnings there if you dig deep enough. A tendency towards self-centredness causes no end of problems, and anything financial will be a nightmare for them to deal with.

MOON IN TAURUS

Sun in Aries (21 Mar. – 20 Apr.)   A confident exterior yet a stubborn streak a mile wide. This person is lovable because of the enthusiasm they have for nearly everything. There may be inner struggles going on here, because the Aries Sun needs space, and the Taurus Moon demands closeness.

Sun in Taurus (21 Apr. – 21 May)   Lots of fixed ideas, very dogmatic but loyal, this person can be a little too materialistic and inflexible, but will be very loving all the same. Likely to be very possessive and very jealous, this person needs lots of hugs, affection and sex.

Sun in Gemini (22 May – 21 June)   Homely, patient and loving, this is a person who is likely to be a good and effective communicator, with lots of ideas and energy. Not always loyal themselves, they expect loyalty from their partner, due to conflict between the Sun and Moon placements.

Sun in Cancer (22 June – 23 July)   Both signs are very home-loving, needing security at all costs, and this feature will be enhanced here. Good with money but subject to moodiness, this is a caring and tactile person, who will be quite possessive and jealous. They need a faithful partner who offers emotional security as well as physical passion.

Sun in Leo (24 July – 23 Aug.)   Warm, loving, very fixed in opinions yet family-minded, this is a confident and determined person who will protect the family group, no matter what. Likely to be bossy, this person needs someone who can be flexible.

Sun in Virgo (24 Aug. – 23 Sept.)   Practical and down to earth, this sensible person may have a lack of self-esteem, and be far too materialistic, critical and analytical. These people are often unable to show emotions, although they are not as bad as most Virgo people in this respect.

Sun in Libra (24 Sept. – 23 Oct.)   A great family person with a keen mind, this is someone who seeks perfection in a partner but may need a good push every now and again, being indecisive. Venus rules both signs, so there is a desire for love and sexual intimacy.

Sun in Scorpio (24 Oct. – 22 Nov.)   Reliable and sensual, insecure and possessive, this is someone who could have problems with their Moon placement, sending out conflicting messages of sensuality behind a fixed moral and ethical interior. Jealous, stubborn and highly sexed, this is someone who needs an understanding mate.

Sun in Sagittarius (23 Nov. – 21 Dec.)   Imaginative and good fun, this person will be enthusiastic about new projects, but again may have problems, because their core personality is happy-go-lucky, and their inner self is a little more restrained. Likely to be restless and outspoken, this is another person who can have problems with their Sun and Moon placements.

Sun in Capricorn (22 Dec. – 20 Jan.)   Both very stubborn signs, leading to a person who can be very fixed in views, a bit of a workaholic, pessimistic and traditional, practical and sensible, but above all caring, and quite sensual with the right partner. Security will matter greatly to this person, and they need a stable career.

Sun in Aquarius (21 Jan. – 19 Feb.)   Nothing will get this person down for long. They always seem to bounce back. Reliable and caring, this person is also rather fixed in ideas at times then totally unconventional at others, and may appear distant. This person needs someone who will give them space.

Sun in Pisces (20 Feb. – 20 Mar.)   Procrastination will be a problem with this person, as motivation isn't a strong point. Romance will be there in abundance, however, for the right partner, as this is a very sensitive, tactile person, who needs a lot of support and security.

MOON IN GEMINI

Sun in Aries (21 Mar. – 20 Apr.) This person starts things but often fails to finish. Sharp-tongued yet quick-witted, this is someone who could have problems with relationships, but will definitely make an impact. Critics would say this person loves the sound of their own voice, but they are very charming people, all the same, who need lots of excitement and challenge from a relationship.

Sun in Taurus (21 Apr. – 21 May) Homely and affectionate, this person can be terribly impatient, very serious and take some time to get to know and understand properly. Not one to be rushed, this is someone who will want to talk a lot. Their partner will need to understand their constantly changing moods.

Sun in Gemini (22 May – 21 June) Lots of talk, but maybe too little action, makes this person rather detached from emotional matters and rather childlike. This person is intuitive about others, needs freedom in a relationship, and may indulge in affairs rather than staying in a permanent relationship.

Sun in Cancer (22 June – 23 July) A great business person and talker who may manipulate others. They will be quite sensitive and easily hurt, though at times they shy away from anything overly emotional. Not a very passionate type this.

Sun in Leo (24 July – 23 Aug.) Energetic and always on the go, this dynamic person both thinks quickly and acts with speed. Romantic, loving, sensual and giving, this is a passionate person, who needs tons of attention from someone who is equally active. Watch for the temper though!

Sun in Virgo (24 Aug. – 23 Sept.) Chatty, intelligent, active and analytical, this person often fails to understand themselves or others. There can be problems with the physical side of things, as they seem detached from emotional matters, yet they will worry about everything. They need an exciting partner to get them out of themselves.

Sun in Libra (24 Sept. – 23 Oct.) Fickle and shallow at times, this person needs other people more than most. Charming and magnetic, they will certainly know how to romance a partner, but be highly strung. This person needs someone who will give them space, as they are restless types.

Sun in Scorpio (24 Oct. – 22 Nov.)   Intuitive and quite psychic, this person is cautious in dealings with others. Exceptionally jealous, highly emotional and very possessive, this person will be very tactile and passionate. Problems with Sun and Moon placements can lead this person to be unfaithful, and to be always looking for something which appears out of reach.

Sun in Sagittarius (23 Nov. – 21 Dec.)   Active and chatty, this person is great fun, but is quite likely to cling to past hurts. They need lots of affection and understanding, and yet hate being tied down. This person is complex and sometimes difficult, and may have a temper problem.

Sun in Capricorn (22 Dec. – 20 Jan.)   Organised, methodical, witty and clever, this is someone who could, or should, work in a creative job. Conflicts between Sun and Moon placements may cause them difficulties with relationships, as they are prone to rapid mood changes and may have problems with commitment.

Sun in Aquarius (21 Jan. – 19 Feb.)   Needing lots of stimulation and change, this person is an effective communicator who is always on the move. They will probably dislike any form of commitment, and may fear a one-to-one relationship. It takes time to get to know this person.

Sun in Pisces (20 Feb. – 20 Mar.)   Changeable, talkative, witty and fun, this person worries far too much for their own good, but is very romantic, sensitive and loving. They often have problems staying the course, and won't cope well with pressure.

MOON IN CANCER

Sun in Aries (21 Mar. – 20 Apr.)   Lively and outspoken, determined yet sensitive, this person is a contradiction, because they are partly homely and quiet and partly loud and aggressive. This is someone who needs a generous and understanding partner.

Sun in Taurus (21 Apr. – 21 May)   Loving, caring, warm and compassionate, this is a very sensitive type, who will also be a little unbending, but very family-minded. Jealous, outgoing and chatty, this is a very physical person.

Sun in Gemini (22 May – 21 June) This person is torn at times between responsibilities and freedom, and often between what they want from a relationship and what it actually is. They are likely to be very talkative and communicative, so watch the phone bills.

Sun in Cancer (22 June – 23 July) The double Cancer is a really compassionate, loving family person, but can be terribly moody and emotional. This person really is hypersensitive, easily hurt and discouraged, very sentimental and yet a brilliant provider and business person.

Sun in Leo (24 July – 23 Aug.) Home and family will be of paramount importance to this person, who will be intensely emotional and warm, and feel the need to do everything on a big scale. A great friend and a very kind person.

Sun in Virgo (24 Aug. – 23 Sept.) Problems with moods again here. This is a fussy, somewhat manipulative person, moody but caring, who will be very traditional, practical and flexible, but worry a lot and be very sentimental.

Sun in Libra (24 Sept. – 23 Oct.) Home will be a haven from the storms of the outside world. Sensitive, jealous and often unrealistic, they may have problems making decisions and making enough personal space for themselves.

Sun in Scorpio (24 Oct. – 22 Nov.) Intense, easy to talk to, magnetic, moody, intuitive, passionate, very jealous and unforgiving – well, what a person this is! Great company, until the moods strike, and very easily hurt.

Sun in Sagittarius (23 Nov. – 21 Dec.) Much as with the Gemini Sun and Sagittarius Moon combination this is someone who will be torn between doing their own thing and having responsibilities. Intuitive and loving, there's a tendency here to be a little foolish.

Sun in Capricorn (22 Dec. – 20 Jan.) Security will be of vital importance for this person, both financial and emotional. Career will matter a lot, but there may be little room for fun and enjoyment, and this person may often feel pulled in opposite directions.

Sun in Aquarius (21 Jan. – 19 Feb.) Unconventional yet family-minded, especially good with children, this person will be a little less erratic than most Aquarius people, but likely to be rather withdrawn at times.

Sun in Pisces (20 Feb. – 20 Mar.) Romantic and loving, this is the true charmer of the group. This person should try to be more realistic, less impractical, and less moody. Exceptionally deep emotionally, this person needs a stable home life.

MOON IN LEO

Sun in Aries (21 Mar. – 20 Apr.) This is someone you cannot ignore, however hard you try. Larger than life, bossy, faithful, loving, attractive, dashing, always on the go, this person often fails to think things through, but can be very sensitive underneath that domineering facade.

Sun in Taurus (21 Apr. – 21 May) A difficult combination with opposing feelings causing confusion all round, especially for the person themselves. They are active and loving, stubborn and inflexible, and need a very loving partner.

Sun in Gemini (22 May – 21 June) This person is talkative, witty, exciting, changeable and attention-seeking. They may not always be aware of feelings, whether their own or other people's but they are likely to have a lot of friends. Their attitude to life may be childlike.

Sun in Cancer (22 June – 23 July) Jealous, possessive, moody, and often very difficult, this person likes things their way. A good provider and family person, they may not be easy to live with, and can be easily upset.

Sun in Leo (24 July – 23 Aug.) Easily wounded when faced with the truth of their self-centredness, this is a person whose brash and extrovert exterior hides a soft, witty, romantic and possibly insecure inner self. Subject to mood changes, this person is not easy to live with and needs a flexible and understanding partner.

Sun in Virgo (24 Aug. – 23 Sept.) Hard-working, quite outgoing and determined, this person is great in business and can become married to their job. Likely to be critical yet sensitive, this person can have a problem understanding their own emotions, and be very insecure.

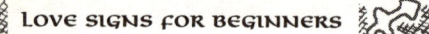

Sun in Libra (24 Sept. – 23 Oct.)   This person loves luxury in a big way, and may find themselves romanticising about other people. Often preoccupied with their appearance, this person is romantic, charming, active and outgoing, yet may find difficulty with their emotions.

Sun in Scorpio (24 Oct. – 22 Nov.)   There is lots of emotion, passion and intensity here, but also stubbornness and awkwardness. This person may have lots of trouble balancing their emotions with their determination to be centre-stage a lot of the time, and is prone to over-react.

Sun in Sagittarius (23 Nov. – 21 Dec.)   Needing freedom and yet wanting attention, this person often has no idea at all about emotional relationships. They can be great fun but can also be crude and tactless.

Sun in Capricorn (22 Dec. – 20 Jan.)   Work is a big part of this person's life, but they make great bosses. Although warm, generous and giving, they may marry for money or status, and may have problems with relationships because of their bossy attitude.

Sun in Aquarius (21 Jan. – 19 Feb.)   There are problems here for this person, who may feel as if they are two different people within one body. They often find themselves in more than one relationship at a time, or else have a series of partners. Active and outgoing, they need a lot of freedom, and can easily cope with several jobs.

Sun in Pisces (20 Feb. – 20 Mar.)   Tending to be rather impractical, especially with money, this loving person is very moody and very gullible. Home and family will be important, but so will love and romance.

MOON IN VIRGO

Sun in Aries (21 Mar. – 20 Apr.)   Shy but sometimes very critical, this individual is very clever but not very outgoing. Prone to insecurity and inner conflict, they need careful handling by a loving partner.

Sun in Taurus (21 Apr. – 21 May)   Chatty, jealous, possessive, pessimistic and often pedantic, this person is very family-oriented.

Lots of passion and strength in this person, who may be very deep and earthy.

Sun in Gemini (22 May – 21 June)   Mercury rules both signs, so there's a lot of talk and ideas with this person. Often lacking in self-esteem, restless and highly strung, this person is very capable and practical, but may have problems showing emotion.

Sun in Cancer (22 June – 23 July)   This person is likely to be moody and easily upset, never forgetting anything, hurts included. They may worry a lot, but will also be very caring. They need a partner who is of a similar nature. Family will matter an awful lot to them.

Sun in Leo (24 July – 23 Aug.)   Industrious and hard-working, determined and stubborn, this person is often difficult to get on with, although they will be very loving. The problem lies with understanding their own emotions.

Sun in Virgo (24 Aug. – 23 Sept.)   The double Virgo will have low self-confidence, be somewhat of a workaholic, analyse all the time, worry about anything and everything, and be rather prudish. However, they will also be very loving and giving.

Sun in Libra (24 Sept. – 23 Oct.)   Sensible, loyal, loving and family-minded, this quiet, dignified person loves the finer things of life but not its rougher edges. They need a trouble-free and orderly life with a partner who will teach them to enjoy themselves.

Sun in Scorpio (24 Oct. – 22 Nov.)   Giving and trusting, extremely sensitive, intense and deep, this person is likely to mother people, irrespective of gender, often falling foul of their own generous nature. However, they can be very possessive, and an explosive temper lurks beneath their surface.

Sun in Sagittarius (23 Nov. – 21 Dec.)   Often dogmatic, harsh, dictatorial and opinionated, this person none the less means well. They are rather enigmatic and will worry all the time.

Sun in Capricorn (22 Dec. – 20 Jan.)   This double earth sign individual needs security, tradition and stability. Likely to work hard, they find it difficult to relax or play, and can have very limited horizons. They should try to overcome their inhibitions and have fun once in a while.

Sun in Aquarius (21 Jan. – 19 Feb.)   Difficult, idealistic, fussy and pedantic, this person's relationship problems stem from an inability to communicate feelings. Their behaviour may be erratic, and they take a lot of getting to know.

Sun in Pisces (20 Feb. – 20 Mar.)   Another set of opposing zodiac influences. 'Stop worrying and get on with things', is what you feel like saying to this person, who is often better alone than with others. Needing a lot of support, this person is, all the same, very loving and caring, but likely to be easily swayed by the prospect of a more glamorous partner.

Moon in Libra

Sun in Aries (21 Mar. – 20 Apr.)   Loving and caring, but determined to get to the top, this person appears a lot more confident than they really are. Their emotional confusion means they need a lot of careful handling.

Sun in Taurus (21 Apr. – 21 May)   This person is basically lovable and romantic (both signs are ruled by Venus) but they can also be very possessive, conventional and very unadventurous. A person of contradictions who sends out mixed messages.

Sun in Gemini (22 May – 21 June)   Overly talkative, restless and changeable, this fun-loving person can be an awful flirt, and has lots of ideas but doesn't always follow through. They may have problems being faithful, but will certainly have magnetism.

Sun in Cancer (22 June – 23 July)   Family and home will matter a lot to this person, as will harmony and peace, but they may prefer elegant socialising to staying at home. Not able to cope well with difficulties, and being very moody, this person often needs a stronger partner.

Sun in Leo (24 July – 23 Aug.)   This combination makes for lots of panache, charm, sentimentality, sensuality and magnetism. This person can also be domineering, but will always look on the bright side of life. A luxury lifestyle is expected as a matter of course by this person, who will always be on the go.

Sun in Virgo (24 Aug. – 23 Sept.)   Often obsessed with detail, this person may not make much headway in business or in love, because they have difficulty making decisions. Likely to come across as just a bit too perfect, they need a partner who will show them how to let go.

Sun in Libra (24 Sept. – 23 Oct.)   This double Libran will never make up their mind, however long you give them. Likely to prefer the easy life, this person often needs a good push, but is a loyal friend who will often give far too much of their time and effort to help other people.

Sun in Scorpio (24 Oct. – 22 Nov.)   Career will matter a lot to this person, and they are determined to be successful. This is someone you can't ignore, who will be very passionate and overwhelming, but who may have problems balancing feelings with needs.

Sun in Sagittarius (23 Nov. – 21 Dec.)   Although judgemental and often difficult, this person has tons of energy and optimism, and is likely to very ambitious. Talkative and friendly, this person needs a partner whom they can respect.

Sun in Capricorn (22 Dec. – 20 Jan)   A need for stability, inherent materialism and love of the finer things of life makes this person very career-minded and a very hard worker. Likely to be rather a snob, this practical person can often change their views because of pressure from other people.

Sun in Aquarius (21 Jan. – 19 Feb.)   Although fun-loving, great company and a good friend, this person isn't always very reliable, and will always be looking for new experiences and new challenges. This is a difficult person to live with, who takes a lot of understanding.

Sun in Pisces (20 Feb. – 20 Mar.)   Lacking in courage at times and likely to day-dream a lot, this thoughtful and loving person needs a lot of support from a partner. Rather snobbish at times, they may also have problems with physical intimacy and with their nerves.

MOON IN SCORPIO

Sun in Aries (21 Mar. – 20 Apr.)   Tons of energy and passion, making for a real handful. This is the person who can't switch off, will always be on the go, likely to have lots of relationships and who will be very fixed in vision. This person needs someone who is a little unconventional.

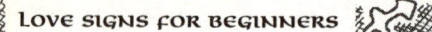

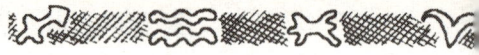

Sun in Taurus (21 Apr. – 21 May) Possessive, jealous, sexy, tactile and loving, this person works hard to get what they want. Not one to share the limelight, they come across as a cauldron of passion beneath a calm exterior, and need a lot of personal space and understanding.

Sun in Gemini (22 May – 21 June) This person is charming, witty, talkative, passionate and magnetic. However, they are also likely to be flighty, insecure, easily hurt, and secretive. They are on a quest to find that perfect partner. Beware of upsetting them, because they can wound with words. What's more, they never forgive or forget.

Sun in Cancer (22 June – 23 July) Moody, jealous, secretive, determined, intuitive and intense, this person will be awash with emotions and sensitivities, and will certainly be someone you notice. They tend to worry and become down-hearted, despite an optimistic exterior. It takes time to know when they are upset, because it just doesn't show.

Sun in Leo (24 July – 23 Aug.) Ambitious, honest, charming and loving, this passionate and unpredictable individual will be hard to ignore. Grand and proud, they will work hard and play hard, but woe betide anyone who upsets them.

Sun in Virgo (24 Aug. – 23 Sept.) Although perhaps a little cold on the surface, this is really a passionate person who needs to be encouraged to relax and let out their emotions. They are caring and loving with the right person, and they love to look after others.

Sun in Libra (24 Sept. – 23 Oct.) Charming, polite and yet sensual and determined, this person can be difficult to fathom. Sexy and deep, they can be rather bossy, very jealous, and slow to forget hurts.

Sun in Scorpio (24 Oct. – 22 Nov.) A double Scorpio is someone who will be so emotional that it may be difficult for them to keep control. Secretive, manipulative, difficult to reach at times and self-protective, a tendency to ride roughshod over people makes this person either a great friend and lover or a terrible enemy.

Sun in Sagittarius (23 Nov. – 21 Dec.) A happy-go-lucky person with lots of passion which can be channelled productively or not, depending on the situation. They are likely to be hard on themselves and others, and can become quite moody when people upset them. This person needs a real individual as a partner.

Sun in Capricorn (22 Dec. – 20 Jan.) A difficult combination with the need for restraint battling with the need to be emotionally open. Likely to be determined, intense and focused, this person will not mince words, and be very secretive, self-protective and ambitious.

Sun in Aquarius (21 Jan. – 19 Feb.) Mixed messages here from the person who seems in control but often isn't and who is very intense and highly emotional. This person appears to be confident, but is also stubborn and doesn't always consider the feelings and needs of others. They may shy away from commitments and one-to-one relationships.

Sun in Pisces (20 Feb. – 20 Mar.) Though romantic, warm, deep, sensual and loving, this person can also be a manipulative and unpredictable day-dreamer who is difficult to live with, self-absorbed and over-sensitive. They need someone realistic to bring them down to earth.

MOON IN SAGITTARIUS

Sun in Aries (21 Mar. – 20 Apr.) Two fire signs make for passion, energy and sparkle, but also impulsiveness and rashness. This person will have problems with relationships, being naturally stubborn, often tactless and cutting, and in need of an awful lot of space. They should think more before they speak.

Sun in Taurus (21 Apr. – 21 May) A difficult combination that embodies opposing needs, so that this person often feels pulled in separate directions. Taurus needs security; Sagittarius need freedom. This person can be very restless, yet a lot of fun.

Sun in Gemini (22 May – 21 June) Fun-loving, witty, magnetic and attractive, yet unlikely to stay still for long, this talkative and active person may be a bit of a flirt, and have little understanding of their own or other people's emotional needs. They really fear commitment.

Sun in Cancer (22 June – 23 July) Another difficult combination, with the Cancer side of the person needing home, family and security and the Sagittarian side needing space and freedom. This person will be good company, need excitement and be very romantic.

Sun in Leo (24 July – 23 Aug.) Passionate and giving, this person is likely to be very loving but need a lot of personal space and be forever on the move, needing a partner who understands this to make for a good relationship. There may be problems making commitments, and they need to learn how to relax.

Sun in Virgo (24 Aug. – 23 Sept.) A caring person who genuinely wants to help others, but who can be a little insensitive on occasion and say things at the wrong time. This person certainly knows how to talk. Once in a relationship, they may be inclined to stray.

Sun in Libra (24 Sept. – 23 Oct.) This person knows what sort of person they are looking for, and will not mind travelling round the world to find them. Charming and witty, they make ideal companions but won't be in one place for long.

Sun in Scorpio (24 Oct. – 22 Nov.) Intense and very intuitive, this person can be very jealous, and have a brilliant sense of humour. Emotional and very moody at times, this person will be difficult to live with and have a terrible temper.

Sun in Sagittarius (23 Nov. – 21 Dec.) A double Sagittarius makes for someone who will rarely stay still long enough to make long-term friendships, and who will not suffer fools gladly. This person will have lots of friends but may not feel the need for a special person. They have problems with commitment.

Sun in Capricorn (22 Dec. – 20 Jan.) The Sagittarian Moon reduces the negative traits of the Capricorn, making for a good friend, who is reliable, friendly, witty, energetic, solid and loyal, and less pessimistic than most Sun Capricorns. This person needs someone who won't mind them working late.

Sun in Aquarius (21 Jan. – 19 Feb.) Fun-loving and yet very unpredictable, this is an impulsive, talkative person who will be great company but a little too honest at times. This person really needs an understanding partner who will give them space.

Sun in Pisces (20 Feb. – 20 Mar.)   Romantic, deep, loving and very intuitive, this person will love travel, but will often have problems with relationships because they feel torn in different directions, both needing and fearing commitment.

MOON IN CAPRICORN

Sun in Aries (21 Mar. – 20 Apr.)   Ambitious, determined and a little aloof, this is a very determined person who may be an enigma and find emotional matters difficult to deal with, coming across as very dogmatic at times.

Sun in Taurus (21 Apr. – 21 May)   Insecurities abound here. This person will work hard, be very serious, and may feel themselves unworthy in the romance stakes. Loving and warm when in the right relationship, this person is good in business and very ambitious, if a little shy.

Sun in Gemini (22 May – 21 June)   Needing more security than most Geminis, this person is very ambitious, great at communication, but not in touch with their emotions. Serious and with a low self-esteem, they need a partner who can show them what fun it can be to discard their inhibitions.

Sun in Cancer (22 June – 23 July)   Two opposite signs here, making for someone who will be very security-minded and very loving, but who will never feel totally relaxed with emotional matters or admit to their needs. Not likely to feel satisfied with anything, this highly intuitive person really works hard, and may be frugal with money.

Sun in Leo (24 July – 23 Aug.)   Charming and grand, yet very insecure and lacking in confidence, this person can often come across as bossy and domineering, but is really warm, romantic and loving underneath that harder exterior, but yet is very stubborn.

Sun in Virgo (24 Aug. – 23 Sept.)   Pessimistic and nervous, conscientious and serious, this exceptionally traditional person will work hard but not know how to play. Materialistic and lacking in vision, this person needs a stable career in order to feel secure, but will be a great family person.

Sun in Libra (24 Sept. – 23 Oct.)   Torn in different directions, this person may be very materialistic, have great judgement and diplomacy where others are concerned. They may also be very deep, seeking constantly for real personal fulfilment.

Sun in Scorpio (24 Oct. – 22 Nov)   Ambitious, serious and determined, this person will get to the top or die trying, A strong and magnetic personality, this person can use others in their quest for success, and will spend far too much time in work-related matters, which means they can end up alone.

Sun in Sagittarius (23 Nov. – 21 Dec.)   Determined and hard-working, this person is very passionate underneath what can appear to be a totally unconcerned exterior. This relatively optimistic person sends out mixed messages, and may never really understand themselves. They are likely to travel a lot, and to lack patience.

Sun in Capricorn (22 Dec. – 20 Jan.)   Far too immersed in business rather than pleasure, this person doesn't know how to switch off, and may be quite happy following career rather than personal goals. Not openly emotional but very practical, this shy person needs someone who can provide some fun and bring them out a bit. There's a lot of deep emotion hidden away.

Sun in Aquarius (21 Jan. – 19 Feb.)   This person may be very unemotional and serious, because they just don't know how to handle emotions. Ambitious and yet lacking in self-confidence, they may find it easier to follow instructions than to take responsibility themselves. A great family person, somewhat unpredictable, but interesting.

Sun in Pisces (20 Feb. – 20 Mar.)   Secretive, deep, serious, romantic yet a worrier, this sensitive person finds problems with relationships because they can't laugh at others or at themselves, and in work because they lack confidence. Very intuitive underneath it all though.

MOON IN AQUARIUS

Sun in Aries (21 Mar. – 20 Apr.)   This somewhat tactless person may never really know or understand what they want from a relationship. Unconventional, amusing, friendly yet obsessional, they get something then want to abandon it for something (or someone) else. Lovable and highly exciting, this person is rarely without a partner for long.

Sun in Taurus (21 Apr. – 21 May)   Changeable and stubborn, this confident person will be very inflexible and really needs a partner who is easy-going and very different. A need for security within a broad spectrum of freedom gives this person an air of mystery.

Sun in Gemini (22 May – 21 June)   Lots of talk, lots of laughter but little emotional depth here. A preference for groups of people rather than one-to-one relationships means this person can be a bit of a difficult catch and need a lot of reassurance. They seem to be really afraid of their own emotions.

Sun in Cancer (22 June – 23 July)   Another difficult combination with needs and feelings never seeming to follow the same course. Likely to need continuous escape routes, either mental or actual, this person may be far too dreamy to cope with the difficulties of ongoing relationships and be far too unpredictable behind a calm exterior. Always on the look-out for opportunities for self-advancement.

Sun in Leo (24 July – 23 Aug.)   A true free spirit, this person won't want to be tied down or restricted, and will be outrageously unconventional at times. Warm and loving, this loyal person can be very difficult, and partners may find them hard to understand and very stubborn.

Sun in Virgo (24 Aug. – 23 Sept.)   Happy in crowds and with groups rather than in a one-to-one relationship, this intense person is very controlled and can appear too practical to be fun. They sit in corners to observe, rather than taking part, and may find themselves being very critical of prospective partners.

Sun in Libra (24 Sept. – 23 Oct.)   A lot of air here, both signs being ruled by that element. This makes for a thinking, independent, highly imaginative person who will hate restrictions and need luxury, and be rather unemotional, but very charming and quite romantic deep down.

Sun in Scorpio (24 Oct. – 22 Nov.)   Lots of difficulties here, due to totally different influences. This strong-willed person comes across as a total enigma and needs freedom yet support, is very passionate and loving, but will come across as rather aloof and hard at times.

Sun in Sagittarius (23 Nov. – 21 Dec.)   Constantly on the go, a great companion and a lot of fun, this very modern and rather eccentric person is optimistic and exciting, but will shy away from commitment.

Sun in Capricorn (22 Dec. – 20 Jan.)   This person has problems showing emotion. Analytical, and very critical of themselves, this person is a good organiser and needs security, but can be very unpredictable. Partners may never fully understand them.

Sun in Aquarius (21 Jan. – 19 Feb.)   Independent, witty, outrageous, this highly nervous person is likely to need a lot of free space, and may not want to have the bother of a relationship. A prospective partner must be prepared for the unexpected, as this is the most eccentric combination imaginable.

Sun in Pisces (20 Feb. – 20 Mar.)   Nobody will ever understand this person, least of all themselves. They live in a purely mental sphere, start things but don't finish them, have little grasp of deep emotional matters outside day-dreams, but love to help other people. Very sensitive, this person needs someone who can make dreams come true.

MOON IN PISCES

Sun in Aries (21 Mar. – 20 Apr.)   Confident on the outside but insecure and exceptionally sensitive on the inside, this person can be very dogmatic, but will mean well all the same. Likely to be very dramatic, this person needs romance in big doses, and can be a very confusing partner.

Sun in Taurus (21 Apr. – 21 May)   Loving, romantic, tactile, warm and considerate, this person dreams and plans for the security they need, but finds it difficult to move forward. Fearing hurts and rejection more than most, they need someone who will listen to their worries and be supportive.

Sun in Gemini (22 May – 21 June)   Talkative and sharing, this person can be a bit of a gossip, a big flirt, highly strung, and won't be able to cope with too many difficulties. Fearing rejection as well as commitment, this person may never be satisfied with what they have, and day-dream all the time.

Sun in Cancer (22 June – 23 July)   This person needs to look after other people as a first priority, and will give of themselves to the last. Loving, warm, sensitive and intuitive, this individual can also be very moody and prone to worry. They need someone who can help stabilise all these emotions. One thing they can offer in return is the practicality to turn dreams into solid reality.

Sun in Leo (24 July – 23 Aug.)   Warm and giving, this extremely deep and sensitive person can become very depressed, but still take on the worries of the world, probably because they need to be needed. Few people will ever completely understand this rather moody and temperamental person.

Sun in Virgo (24 Aug. – 23 Sept.)   Sometimes too caring, thoughtful and altruistic for their own good, this person is likely to be very intuitive and to neglect their own needs. Critical of others, this person worries about most things and is often very restless and shy.

Sun in Libra (24 Sept. – 23 Oct.)   Romantic, passionate and intuitive, this person often thinks too long before acting. They can be a great partner once they've made their mind up, and they stick like glue. They need a partner who will want to stay with them for ever.

Sun in Scorpio (24 Oct. – 22 Nov.)   Moody and intense, this is a private person who none the less needs to give to others. Their magnetism and charm make them difficult to ignore or resist. This is someone awash with sensitivities, emotions and passion.

Sun in Sagittarius (23 Nov. – 21 Dec.)   Impractical, talkative, intuitive and kind, this person loves to help others, and will love travel. Romantic, loving and sensitive, this is an exciting and fun person who is subject to rapid mood changes.

Sun in Capricorn (22 Dec. – 20 Jan.)   This is a serious, intuitive compassionate and loving individual whose hidden depths are difficult to plumb. They are also very practical. People may think there's no emotion there, but there is once the Capricorn feels secure.

Sun in Aquarius (21 Jan. – 19 Feb.) Likely to be interested in anything unusual or mystical, this person is very imaginative and a bit of a dreamer. Intuitive and unpredictable, this is an ideas person who will be very active and very sensitive, although you may never know it.

Sun in Pisces (20 Feb. – 20 Mar.) The double Pisces is very intuitive and impressionable, fears getting hurt more than most, and will know what you are thinking without having to try. A great dreamer, this volatile person is very giving of themselves, often to the detriment of their own well-being.

We are now nearing the end of our journey of discovery, and are getting close to the point of returning back to base, hopefully a little more knowledgeable than when we started. Before moving on to the last chapter, however, see if you can answer these questions.

PRACTICE

- Moon in Leo, Sun in Pisces. What would you expect this person to be like?
- Give two combinations which could prove difficult for this Moon–Leo, Sun–Pisces person.
- The double Leo person will be shy, retiring and unemotional. True or false?
- What would you expect a Cancer Sun and Scorpio Moon person to be like emotionally?
- Back to basics – which sign comes before Scorpio?
- Gemini people are very chatty and communicative. What sort of combination would Gemini Sun with Sagittarius Moon give?

4 COMPATIBILITY

We have looked both at ourselves and at other people through the vehicle of Moon and Sun signs. We have also looked at emotions and emotional compatibilities through Moon placements. But will this enable us to find or create a happy relationship? The answer is yes and no. We will be better placed now to understand our own emotions and those of a partner. However, only a full natal chart will give us a complete picture of our personality, and then we would have to compare it with our partner's chart. Having said this, Sun and Moon placements are perhaps the strongest factors in a birth chart, and will take us a long way in the right direction.

Bearing this in mind, we will now look at pure Sun sign compatibilities, not taking into account the Moon or other planetary placings. This will give us a starting-point from which to look at one person's Moon placement in relation to another's Sun sign.

SUN SIGN COMPATIBILITY

In an earlier chapter we considered one theory relating to compatible signs, based on moving forwards and backwards from a sign, but we are now going to look at how the Sun signs relate to one another, using the following chart. In some cases, as we will have already realised, compatible Moons can and do alter some of the basic Sun sign compatibilities.

There is further information on compatibilities in the partnership section of each sign in my *Star Signs for Beginners*.

General Compatibilities

♀/♂	ARIES	TAURUS	GEMINI	CANCER	LEO	VIRGO	LIBRA	SCORPIO	SAGITTARIUS	CAPRICORN	AQUARIUS	PISCES
ARIES	3	1	3	6	1	3	1	1*	2	2	3	6
TAURUS	2	2	5	3	1*	2	1	2	6	1	1	2
GEMINI	3	4	4	6	2	5	1*	3	3	5	4	6
CANCER	5	2	6	1*	5	3	5	6	4	2	5	6
LEO	3	1	1*	1	5	5	2	3	2	5	4	5
VIRGO	6	2	1	4	4	5	4	1	3	2	5	1*
LIBRA	4	1	1	4	2	5	5	3	3	6	1*	2
SCORPIO	2	3	5	1	2	2	2	3	4	2	4	1*
SAGITTARIUS	1*	4	3	5	2	2	2	5	2	6	5	5
CAPRICORN	3	3	5	1	5	4	5	1	6	1	1*	1
AQUARIUS	2	4	4	5	2	5	1*	4	3	4	1	5
PISCES	4	1	3	2	2	3	1	2	5	1	5	1*

Key to the codes

- 1* = The best
- 1 = Very good/passionate
- 2 = Good
- 3 = Maybe
- 4 = Will need working on
- 5 = No
- 6 = Disastrous

We now need to look at how a person's Moon placement relates to another person's Sun placement. We already have a lot of information on both Sun and Moon signs, and so the information given here will be relatively brief. However, it should suffice to give you a further insight into whether you are likely to gel with a potential partner or not.

Moon and Sun sign compatibility

Moon in Aries

With Sun in Aries A good chance of success. Both people will understand each other, and there's a lot of excitement and activity.
With Sun in Taurus Not a brilliant combination. Too slow and solid for the Aries Moon. Boredom could creep in at an early stage.
With Sun in Gemini Could work. Lots of activity and excitement, but both parties will have to make time together.
With Sun in Cancer Lots of mood swings in the Cancerian makes for hard going at times, but this could work well eventually.
With Sun in Leo Lots of fire but maybe a little too much stress coping with one another for this to work well.
With Sun in Virgo Not a good combination. Their worrying would really get you down in a big way, and they are far too fussy for you.
With Sun in Libra A lack of action makes this a dull relationship, although the Libran will try really hard to make it work.
With Sun in Scorpio Lots of differences, but this could work, although neither party will ever totally understand the other.
With Sun in Sagittarius A great combination. Lots of excitement, activity, talk and space for both parties.
With Sun in Capricorn This would be better as a working partnership than as a relationship. Lots of differences would make it hard going at home.

With Sun in Aquarius Possibilities here, but sometimes Moon in Aries may feel that the Aquarius is all talk and no action, and that will irritate.

With Sun in Pisces The Pisces will be frightened to death by the Aries Moon, and probably won't want a relationship anyway.

MOON IN TAURUS

With Sun in Aries Not a good combination. Moon in Taurus needs far more security, Sun in Aries more excitement.

With Sun in Taurus Lots of similarities, lots of love, affection, hugs and kisses. Great relationship.

With Sun in Gemini Gemini is far too flighty for Taurus and would never keep still long enough. Taurus would be left feeling insecure.

With Sun in Cancer A good team who work well together most of the time, although Taurus could have problems understanding Cancerian moods.

With Sun in Leo Lots of difficulties but few similarities. This relationship could have an initial attraction but then peter out.

With Sun in Virgo A good relationship. Both will support each other and strengths and weaknesses will balance out.

With Sun in Libra Libra, as usual, will try hard to make this work, but it could be difficult for the Taurus Moon, because Librans aren't physical types.

With Sun in Scorpio Possibilities here, but lots of differences, and maybe neither party would understand the other.

With Sun in Sagittarius Not really. Taurus is too possessive for Sagittarius; Sagittarius is too impractical for Taurus.

With Sun in Capricorn Lots of similarities and a good chance of success, once the Capricorn switched off from work and learnt how to cuddle.

With Sun in Aquarius Far too many differences. These people seem to belong on different planets at times. Aquarius is far too eccentric for Taurus.

With Sun in Pisces This could work, but equally it might not. If both worked at it this would stay the course, although the Taurus Moon wouldn't understand the Pisces.

MOON IN GEMINI

With Sun in Aries   Yes, this could work. Lots of talking, lots of fun and a few arguments, though they would probably be quickly forgotten.

With Sun in Taurus   Far too boring for the Gemini Moon. This relationship is the Gemini Moon best left totally alone. You would feel trapped.

With Sun in Gemini   A great relationship with lots of talking, lots of activity and lots of love.

With Sun in Cancer   The Gemini Moon could feel attracted to the loving qualities of the Cancerian but find the restrictions of home life and their moods too much to cope with.

With Sun in Leo   Leo might be too bossy for Moon in Gemini but there would certainly be a lot of warmth here – although lots of arguments too.

With Sun in Virgo   Lots of energy, which means it could work well. Lots of chat but Moon in Gemini might irritate Virgo.

With Sun in Libra   This could work. Both have qualities which the other respects, but sometimes Libra would seem too staid for the Gemini Moon.

With Sun in Scorpio   Lots of differences but sometimes these can prove attractive, and Scorpio people certainly have a lot of magnetism.

With Sun in Sagittarius   Opposites attract, and this may be the case here. Lots of freedom to move around and lots of talking, so maybe.

With Sun in Capricorn   A partnership which should perhaps be a working one rather than a loving one. Both strive for similar things but Capricorn is very serious, and the Gemini Moon would feel stifled sometimes.

With Sun in Aquarius   A great combination. Both are wild and wacky, and there would be lots to talk about, lots of space and lots of action.

With Sun in Pisces   Moon in Gemini might find Pisces too dreamy. This relationship could work but it would be a challenge, and there might not be a lot of closeness.

MOON IN CANCER

With Sun in Aries   Too many differences here. There may be an attraction, but the whole thing would be very problematical.

With Sun in Taurus   Lots of home comforts and family life, but not a lot of action, although lots of cuddles. A maybe.

With Sun in Gemini   Not really a good relationship. Too much activity and too little emotion shown. The Moon in Cancer would feel really insecure.

With Sun in Cancer   Yes. A great pairing who appreciate each other's needs, will love each other and work well to iron out the day's problems.

With Sun in Leo   A possibility, but a lot of hard work needed. Moon in Cancer might find Leo domineering and insensitive, while Leo might have problems with Moon in Cancer's moods.

With Sun in Virgo   Lots of similarities, lots of shared interests and a lot of security, but maybe too many worries at times. A possibility.

With Sun in Libra   Both need a comfortable and stable home life, and neither like arguments, so this would work, although it could be a little dull.

With Sun in Scorpio   Lots of emotion here – maybe too much at times. Mismatched moods could cause problems.

With Sun in Sagittarius   Not really. Sagittarius is far too active, impractical and tactless for Moon in Cancer, while Moon in Cancer is too easily wounded for Sagittarius.

With Sun in Capricorn   Both value security, tradition and home, but Capricorn wouldn't understand Moon in Cancer moods, and Moon in Cancer wouldn't like Capricorn's workaholic tendencies.

With Sun in Aquarius   Not at all. Aquarius is far too avant garde and embarrassing for Moon in Cancer.

With Sun in Pisces   A great complementary team. Lots of love, romance, hugs and kisses, and a really stable home life.

MOON IN LEO

With Sun in Aries   A 50–50 chance of success. Lots of action, but there could be just too much competition for Moon in Leo to feel secure.

With Sun in Taurus Not enough action, too little flexibility on both sides, and very little excitement. This wouldn't work well.

With Sun in Gemini Gemini may be a little too changeable and tactless at times for Moon in Leo, but this could work because there are similar traits.

With Sun in Cancer There could be power struggles, because Moon in Leo requires a lot of attention and may not respect the Cancerian's needs. A 'maybe' relationship.

With Sun in Leo A great team here. Both understand each other and will work well. A lot of warmth and passion, and a lot of love.

With Sun in Virgo Virgo will irritate Moon in Leo by their nit-picking, worrying ways, though at least Moon in Leo won't have to worry about being upstaged. Not really a good relationship.

With Sun in Libra A good relationship. The flexible Libra will give the Moon in Leo the attention they need and provide a stable and happy home base.

With Sun in Scorpio Scorpio needs to be in control and will try to manipulate. Moon in Leo will hate that.

With Sun in Sagittarius Sagittarians need a lot of space, and can be very insensitive, and could wound Moon in Leo's pride. Lots of attraction though.

With Sun in Capricorn Both work hard, like similar things and value traditional standards, although in the passion stakes it might be a little dull.

With Sun in Aquarius Aquarians are far too flighty and up in the air for Moon in Leo, and would drive them positively mental. Neither would give an inch.

With Sun in Pisces Moon in Leo will have to be very tolerant of the Piscean whims and ideals for this to last. Pisces will try very hard though.

MOON IN VIRGO

With Sun in Aries This isn't a good combination, because both are essentially very different, need different things and work in different ways.

With Sun in Taurus A good combination, but not one with a lot of initiative at times. Both admire, respect and understand each other.

With Sun in Gemini   Both can work well together, but little things might irritate Moon in Virgo, and Gemini will hate the Virgoan need for tidiness.

With Sun in Cancer   Moon in Virgo may not understand Cancerian moods, and will upset them for ages if they say so. This would need a lot of mutual understanding.

With Sun in Leo   Not a good match. Moon in Virgo would never understand Leo's needs and behaviour.

With Sun in Virgo   Great. Both work hard towards the same goals but maybe there needs to be a third party to get some action going.

With Sun in Libra   Libra will try really hard to make sure this works, and it may do if Moon in Virgo tries not to find fault too much.

With Sun in Scorpio   Scorpios are very magnetic and intense, and although Moon in Virgo would probably try hard, this isn't a good combination.

With Sun in Sagittarius   Sagittarians never sit still, tidy up after themselves or finish one thing before starting another – unlike Moon in Virgo. A big no.

With Sun in Capricorn   Possibly a good match, although the Moon in Virgo might find that the Capricorn wasn't home as much as they'd like, and that they were a little intolerant at times.

With Sun in Aquarius   Not at all. Nothing in common and the Aquarian won't stay around for Moon in Virgo to even think about tidying up after them.

With Sun in Pisces   Pisceans are too dreamy and impractical for Moon in Virgo. They aren't tidy either – but they would try hard.

Moon in Libra

With Sun in Aries   The Moon in Libra person just wouldn't feel comfortable around the Aries for long. Not a good relationship, even with a lot of effort.

With Sun in Taurus   This combination might be too solid and dull for Moon in Libra. Although there could be lots of good points, it would be difficult physically.

With Sun in Gemini   Potential here for a relationship, but a lot of differences. Gemini may be too wacky for Moon in Libra to cope with for long.

With Sun in Cancer Cancer's moods can cause Moon in Libra a lot of problems, but Cancers really do care deeply for their partners. Given the will, this will work.

With Sun in Leo Both expect the finest, and make a good team in this respect. Leo will always be boss, but Moon in Libra may not mind, so it could work.

With Sun in Virgo A reasonable pairing, but a little lacking in passion. Both understand each other, but there won't be many parties.

With Sun in Libra A great match. Both like similar things and will get on together well, unless there's a big emotional problem, when neither will be able to deal with it.

With Sun in Scorpio Scorpios are very sexual, and that won't sit well with Moon in Libra. Neither will their emotional behaviour. Not a good match.

With Sun in Sagittarius If the Moon in Libra can cope with the Sagittarian's tactlessness and need to have their own circle of friends, this could work fine.

With Sun in Capricorn Not a lot of emotion but this could work, as both like similar things. It would need a lot of hard work though.

With Sun in Aquarius After a promising start, this relationship will fall by the wayside. Moon in Libra just can't cope with Aquarius.

With Sun in Pisces Maybe this could work. Home life will be stable and loving, but there won't be much excitement, and Pisces may be a little too impractical for Moon in Libra.

MOON IN SCORPIO

With Sun in Aries Not a good idea. Too many differences, leading to lots of conflict, arguments and stress for both parties.

With Sun in Taurus Lots of passion, warmth and feeling, but both go about things in different ways and are unlikely to change – especially the Taurus.

With Sun in Gemini Lots of attraction but maybe too much activity and change for Moon in Scorpio's liking long-term, and

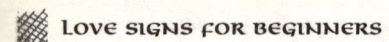

Gemini would hate the restrictions Moon in Scorpio would place on them.

With Sun in Cancer   Both signs will help each other, and this could work. Emotionally very similar in many respects, they will certainly be supportive.

With Sun in Leo   This is not a good relationship. Leo's pompous need to be centre-stage all the time would really rub Moon in Scorpio up the wrong way.

With Sun in Virgo   Virgo will try really hard to get this relationship going, but they will irritate Moon in Scorpio and never understand their intensities.

With Sun in Libra   Moon in Scorpio is far too sexual and emotional for the Libran. They work different ways, for different goals. No way.

With Sun in Scorpio   Yes. Lots of passion, sex and emotion. This couple will have problems with each other's jealous nature, but then nothing's perfect!

With Sun in Sagittarius   The Scorpio Moon wouldn't catch the Sagittarius for long enough to find out whether it would work, and believe me, it wouldn't. Too many differences.

With Sun in Capricorn   If the Scorpio Moon can get used to being alone at home a lot, then this relationship might work, although the Scorpio Moon would prefer more passion.

With Sun in Aquarius   Scorpio Moons are too jealous and possessive for Aquarius; Aquarians need more space than the Scorpio Moon would be prepared to give. Apart from that, they don't have much in common anyway.

With Sun in Pisces   The Scorpio Moon would have to give all the time for this to work, and might find it too much like hard work.

MOON IN SAGITTARIUS

With Sun in Aries   Lots of excitement, lots of activity, lots of space for both parties, so this could work.

With Sun in Taurus   Taurus is far too jealous, stubborn and homely for Sagittarius. This relationship is likely to be short-lived.

With Sun in Gemini   Lots of talk, lots of activity, lots of space for both parties, and excitement aplenty. This could work well.

With Sun in Cancer Cancer is too moody and too much of a homebody for the Sagittarian Moon, who needs someone who will give them more personal space then Cancer would be prepared to give.

With Sun in Leo Lots of passion and a very active social life, but the Sagittarian Moon might steal Leo's limelight – and they'd hate that.

With Sun in Virgo Virgo will try really hard to adjust to their partner's needs but they may be a little too unadventurous and anxious for Moon in Sagittarius.

With Sun in Libra This pair will be interested in each other mentally, but the physical side could be a problem, and there won't be much emotion. On the plus side, Libra will allow Moon in Sagittarius to come and go as they wish.

With Sun in Scorpio No chance. Moon in Sagittarius will come to resent Scorpio's behaviour and there would be far too many rows, with neither side backing down.

With Sun in Sagittarius A great match, both understanding the other and working well together to create space. Lots of talk, warmth and love.

With Sun in Capricorn Capricorns are very work-minded, straightforward and serious. Moon in Sagittarius prefers more fun, and is more laid-back and optimistic. Not a good match.

With Sun in Aquarius Lots of talk, fun and activity. Both are highly individual, but both care a great deal. A reasonable match.

With Sun in Pisces This could work if Moon in Sagittarius tries to be a little more sensitive to the Piscean's needs, and a little more tactful.

MOON IN CAPRICORN

With Sun in Aries A 50/50 chance of making it. This relationship is not without problems. Aries may take too many risks for Moon in Capricorn.

With Sun in Taurus A good match this, as both are solid, reliable and loyal, although also very stubborn. Moon in Capricorn would need to relax.

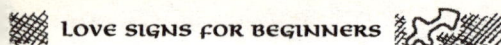

With Sun in Gemini Gemini won't mind Moon in Capricorn working late, and there will be lots of chat, but they may still be too different for a successful relationship.

With Sun in Cancer Both can be moody, and if that happens at the same time, it could cause problems. Both traditionalist and security-minded, this could work.

With Sun in Leo Moon in Capricorn might find it all a bit much. Leos need to have such a lot of attention all the time, but at least Moon in Capricorn would learn to have fun.

With Sun in Virgo Lots in common, but a relationship which would lack passion and sparkle, although they work well together.

With Sun in Libra Lacking in passion, but sustainable, although both could do better.

With Sun in Scorpio Similar drives and aims, but Moon in Capricorn might have problems with Scorpio's physical needs and emotional depths. Could work given time.

With Sun in Sagittarius Not really. The Sagittarius is too freedom-loving, and they would rub each other up the wrong way.

With Sun in Capricorn Two career-minded types can create a tram-lined relationship, with neither party meeting the other often enough.

With Sun in Aquarius Aquarius is a little too way out for Moon in Capricorn, but probably wouldn't notice their being late home from work. Not a good mixture.

With Sun in Pisces This pair could work well together in a supportive and caring way. This relationship would help both to balance out the positive and negative parts of their characters.

MOON IN AQUARIUS

With Sun in Aries Lots of space for both parties, but not a lot of passion, and Moon in Aquarius would find Aries self-centred.

With Sun in Taurus Taureans are too solid and traditional for Moon in Aquarius, who would be bored most of the time and out for the rest of it.

With Sun in Gemini Lots of talk, lots of ideas, lots of space, but perhaps not enough passion or emotion for it to feel worthwhile.

With Sun in Cancer Cancerians like homelife, Moon in Aquarius doesn't. Cancerians are very moody, and Moon in Aquarius wouldn't understand why. Cancerians are easily upset and Moon in Aquarius is very unconventional. Not a good relationship.

With Sun in Leo Leos want everything that is unimportant to Moon in Aquarius. This couple wouldn't get on too well.

With Sun in Virgo Lots of talk, lots of ideas and lots of differences. This could work, because Virgo would try really hard.

With Sun in Libra Libra is a little too staid and prudish for Moon in Aquarius, and would find the Aquarian eccentricity an embarrassment in a lot of cases.

With Sun in Scorpio No chance of this relationship making it to the baseball pitch, let alone past first base. Too many differences by far.

With Sun in Sagittarius This could work well. Sagittarius wouldn't notice their partner's failings and Moon in Aquarius would have lots of space and freedom. Plenty of talk and interests in common.

With Sun in Capricorn Moon in Aquarius would have lots of freedom because Capricorn wouldn't be home much. Capricorn is far too traditional for Aquarius.

With Sun in Aquarius A great relationship if it ever happens. Both are so individual that they might get on really well.

With Sun in Pisces These two aren't on the same wavelength, although they may want similar things. Not a good relationship, because Pisces will need their partner at home more than Moon in Aquarius is prepared to be.

MOON IN PISCES

With Sun in Aries Not in a million years. Moon in Pisces would find Aries far too overpowering to contemplate a relationship.

With Sun in Taurus Taureans are tactile people, physical and sexual, and this could cause problems. However, it could work eventually.

With Sun in Gemini Geminis need a lot of space, move around a lot and change all the time. Moon in Pisces wouldn't really understand this. Not a good relationship, despite a mental attraction.

With Sun in Cancer A great relationship. Both are romantic, emotional and loving, and will understand and meet the other person's need for security.

With Sun in Leo Moon in Pisces won't mind Leo's showy ways and need to be in the limelight, and will bend to accommodate their whims. However, Leo probably won't offer the same in return.

With Sun in Virgo These two will get on well together, even though they may not understand each other. Both will help the other and make a good team.

With Sun in Libra Both will benefit a lot from this relationship, and despite contrary indications, this relationship will work out well.

With Sun in Scorpio Scorpio is a little strong-willed for Moon in Pisces, who might feel steam-rollered and worry too much about their partner's motives.

With Sun in Sagittarius Lots of fun, but a little tactless remark every now and again will really hurt Moon in Pisces and undermine all that has been achieved. Probably not a good match.

With Sun in Capricorn Capricorn will certainly provide security, but not a lot of romance, and they will work exceptionally long hours, thinking of the material security they can provide rather than the wasted hours of passion.

With Sun in Aquarius This relationship looks all right on the surface, but there won't be much emotional security for you, and you may feel left out in the cold.

With Sun in Pisces This is a great relationship between two emotional, sensitive and caring individuals who think and act along the same lines.

In Conclusion

We have now looked at all the Sun/Moon compatibilities, and are nearing the end of our journey. There are many factors which can make or break a relationship, and many facets of personality which this book has not been able to highlight. However, you will by now have learnt a great deal about the emotions that arise in relationships, and you should be able to use this information to advance your understanding of others and how you relate to them.

However, in the end the choice is ours. Sometimes we just have to find out for ourselves, and sometimes we find out the hard way. Other times, with a little forethought and knowledge, we can perhaps avoid the pitfalls. If you are advising others, it is especially important to remember that people often have to find out for themselves, even if you are able to offer guidance.

APPENDIX

FINDING MOON SIGNS

In the tables which follow, all years from 1940 to 1980 are covered. All you need to do is find your date of birth, though it helps if you also know the time. All the times given are based on **Greenwich Mean Time** so please bear this in mind when making your calculations. You then look at the month and date.

Let's take a quick example. Sue was born on 16 June 1955 at 7pm. On that date, the Moon was in Taurus after 6.50am. It remained in Taurus until 7.37am on 18 June, at which time it moved to Gemini. Sue's Moon is therefore in Taurus. Let's take another example. Darren was born on 4 July 1971. He was born at 3am, or 03.00 hours. Looking at the tables, we will see that the Moon came into Sagittarius at 23.59, prior to which it was in Scorpio. As Darren was born at 15.00 hours, his Moon is in Scorpio, not in Sagittarius.

LOVE SIGNS FOR BEGINNERS

—1940—

JAN
Day	Time	Sign
1	10:43	LIB
3	14:36	SCO
5	20:12	SAG
8	3:30	CAP
10	12:42	AQU
13	0:03	PIS
15	12:55	ARI
18	1:15	TAU
20	10:32	GEM
22	15:35	CAN
24	17:10	LEO
26	17:12	VIR
28	17:43	LIB
30	20:17	SCO

FEB
Day	Time	Sign
2	1:36	SAG
4	9:27	CAP
6	19:21	AQU
9	6:58	PIS
11	19:49	ARI
14	8:36	TAU
16	19:10	GEM
19	1:46	CAN
21	4:19	LEO
23	4:11	VIR
25	3:29	LIB
27	4:13	SCO
29	7:54	SAG

MAR
Day	Time	Sign
2	15:02	CAP
5	1:07	AQU
7	13:07	PIS
10	2:01	ARI
12	14:44	TAU
15	1:53	GEM
17	9:57	CAN
19	14:15	LEO
21	15:21	VIR
23	14:47	LIB
25	14:33	SCO
27	16:31	SAG
29	21:59	CAP

APR
Day	Time	Sign
1	7:13	AQU
3	19:11	PIS
6	8:10	ARI
8	20:39	TAU
11	7:32	GEM
13	16:04	CAN
15	21:44	LEO
18	0:34	VIR
20	1:23	LIB
22	1:33	SCO
24	2:48	SAG
26	6:50	CAP
28	14:39	AQU

MAY
Day	Time	Sign
1	1:56	PIS
3	14:52	ARI
6	3:12	TAU
8	13:34	GEM
10	21:33	CAN
13	3:22	LEO
15	7:18	VIR
17	9:40	LIB
19	11:12	SCO
21	13:00	SAG
23	16:34	CAP
25	23:19	AQU
28	9:39	PIS
30	22:18	ARI

JUN
Day	Time	Sign
2	10:44	TAU
4	20:49	GEM
7	4:02	CAN
9	9:00	LEO
11	12:41	VIR
13	15:43	LIB
15	18:32	SCO
17	21:34	SAG
20	1:44	CAP
22	8:15	AQU
24	17:55	PIS
27	6:13	ARI
29	18:52	TAU

JUL
Day	Time	Sign
2	5:15	GEM
4	12:11	CAN
6	16:12	LEO
8	18:44	VIR
10	21:07	LIB
13	0:05	SCO
15	4:05	SAG
17	9:17	CAP
19	16:22	AQU
22	1:58	PIS
24	14:01	ARI
27	2:56	TAU
29	14:04	GEM
31	21:32	CAN

AUG
Day	Time	Sign
3	1:20	LEO
5	2:50	VIR
7	3:50	LIB
9	5:46	SCO
11	9:29	SAG
13	15:15	CAP
15	23:07	AQU
18	9:10	PIS
20	21:14	ARI
23	10:17	TAU
25	22:13	GEM
28	6:53	CAN
30	11:31	LEO

SEP
Day	Time	Sign
3	12:57	VIR
5	12:54	LIB
7	13:16	SCO
9	15:36	SAG
11	20:45	CAP
14	4:51	AQU
16	15:25	PIS
19	3:43	ARI
21	16:45	TAU
24	5:05	GEM
26	14:57	CAN
28	21:09	LEO
30	23:46	VIR

OCT
Day	Time	Sign
2	23:12	LIB
4	23:54	SCO
7	3:28	SAG
9	10:44	CAP
11	21:18	AQU
14	9:50	PIS
16	22:49	ARI
19	10:59	TAU
21	21:18	GEM
24	4:51	CAN
26	9:10	LEO
28	10:37	VIR
30	10:25	LIB

NOV
Day	Time	Sign
1	10:21	SCO
3	12:22	SAG
5	18:03	CAP
8	3:46	AQU
10	16:13	PIS
13	5:13	ARI
15	17:00	TAU
18	2:52	GEM
20	10:38	CAN
22	16:11	LEO
24	19:25	VIR
26	20:44	LIB
28	21:18	SCO
30	22:50	SAG

DEC
Day	Time	Sign
3	3:12	CAP
5	11:35	AQU
7	23:26	PIS
10	12:27	ARI
13	0:08	TAU
15	9:20	GEM
17	16:16	CAN
19	21:35	LEO
22	1:37	VIR
24	4:30	LIB
26	6:36	SCO
28	8:58	SAG
30	13:09	CAP

—1941—

JAN
Day	Time	Sign
1	20:35	AQU
4	7:34	PIS
6	20:28	ARI
9	8:27	TAU
11	17:33	GEM
13	23:39	CAN
16	3:45	LEO
18	7:00	VIR
20	10:04	LIB
22	13:16	SCO
24	17:01	SAG
26	22:06	CAP
29	5:34	AQU
31	16:02	PIS

FEB
Day	Time	Sign
3	4:41	ARI
5	17:09	TAU
8	2:57	GEM
10	9:07	CAN
12	12:21	LEO
14	14:07	VIR
16	15:52	LIB
18	18:37	SCO
20	22:54	SAG
23	5:02	CAP
25	13:18	AQU
27	23:54	PIS

MAR
Day	Time	Sign
2	12:23	ARI
5	1:12	TAU
7	11:59	GEM
9	19:19	CAN
11	22:51	LEO
13	23:51	VIR
16	0:03	LIB
18	1:08	SCO
20	4:25	SAG
22	10:34	CAP
24	19:30	AQU
27	6:39	PIS
29	19:14	ARI

APR
Day	Time	Sign
1	8:06	TAU
3	19:44	GEM
6	4:26	CAN
8	9:21	LEO
10	10:54	VIR
12	10:31	LIB
14	10:07	SCO
16	11:38	SAG
18	16:31	CAP
21	1:07	AQU
23	12:34	PIS
26	1:23	ARI
28	14:11	TAU

MAY
Day	Time	Sign
1	1:56	GEM
3	11:34	CAN
5	18:06	LEO
7	21:11	VIR
9	21:34	LIB
11	21:03	SCO
13	21:16	SAG
16	0:15	CAP
18	7:33	AQU
20	18:34	PIS
23	7:26	ARI
25	20:10	TAU
28	7:36	GEM
30	17:15	CAN

JUN
Day	Time	Sign
2	1:56	LEO
4	5:17	VIR
6	7:13	LIB
8	7:24	SCO
10	7:31	SAG
12	9:41	CAP
14	15:33	AQU
17	1:30	PIS
19	14:03	ARI
22	2:44	TAU
24	13:51	GEM
26	22:55	CAN
29	6:03	LEO

JUL
Day	Time	Sign
1	11:17	VIR
3	14:34	LIB
5	17:21	SCO
7	19:36	SAG
9	0:42	CAP
12	9:35	AQU
14	21:30	PIS
17	10:10	ARI
19	21:15	TAU
22	5:48	GEM
24	12:03	CAN
26	16:41	LEO
28	20:29	VIR
30	19:14	LIB

AUG
Day	Time	Sign
2	22:49	SAG
4	1:17	CAP
6	4:32	AQU
8	9:51	PIS
10	18:13	ARI
13	5:32	TAU
15	18:09	GEM
18	5:37	CAN
20	14:15	LEO
22	19:53	VIR
24	23:21	LIB
27	1:48	SCO
29	4:13	SAG
31	7:18	CAP

SEP
Day	Time	Sign
2	11:39	AQU
4	17:52	PIS
7	2:28	ARI
9	13:32	TAU
12	2:06	GEM
14	14:09	CAN
16	23:36	LEO
19	5:29	VIR
21	8:17	LIB
23	9:24	SCO
25	10:24	SAG
27	12:44	CAP
29	17:17	AQU

OCT
Day	Time	Sign
2	0:18	PIS
4	9:37	ARI
6	20:52	TAU
9	9:23	GEM
11	21:53	CAN
14	8:29	LEO
16	15:36	VIR
18	18:54	LIB
20	19:00	SCO
22	19:25	SAG
24	19:40	CAP
26	23:02	AQU
29	5:51	PIS
31	15:38	ARI

NOV
Day	Time	Sign
3	3:19	TAU
5	15:52	GEM
8	4:26	CAN
10	15:49	LEO
13	0:29	VIR
15	5:22	LIB
17	6:40	SCO
19	5:53	SAG
21	5:11	CAP
23	6:46	AQU
25	12:09	PIS
27	21:26	ARI
30	9:18	TAU

DEC
Day	Time	Sign
2	22:00	GEM
5	10:22	CAN
7	21:43	LEO
10	7:12	VIR
12	13:46	LIB
14	16:51	SCO
16	17:10	SAG
18	16:26	CAP
20	20:33	AQU
22	4:24	PIS
25	15:43	ARI
27	4:27	TAU
30	(end)	GEM

—1942—

JAN
1	16:42	CAN
4	3:32	LEO
6	12:42	VIR
8	19:48	LIB
11	0:24	SCO
13	2:31	SAG
15	3:07	CAP
17	3:52	AQU
19	6:43	PIS
21	13:08	ARI
23	23:18	TAU
26	11:44	GEM
29	0:03	CAN
31	10:37	LEO

FEB
2	18:57	VIR
5	1:18	LIB
7	5:56	SCO
9	9:07	SAG
11	11:19	CAP
13	13:27	AQU
15	16:50	PIS
17	22:46	ARI
20	7:57	TAU
22	19:47	GEM
25	8:15	CAN
27	19:06	LEO

MAR
2	3:06	VIR
4	8:23	LIB
6	11:50	SCO
8	14:28	SAG
10	17:08	CAP
12	20:30	AQU
15	1:09	PIS
17	7:41	ARI
19	16:39	TAU
22	4:00	GEM
24	16:33	CAN
27	4:04	LEO
29	12:37	VIR
31	17:36	LIB

APR
2	19:54	SCO
4	21:04	SAG
6	22:41	CAP
9	1:56	AQU
11	7:19	PIS
13	14:49	ARI
16	0:18	TAU
18	11:37	GEM
21	0:10	CAN
23	12:21	LEO
25	22:03	VIR
28	3:50	LIB
30	5:59	SCO

MAY
2	6:03	SAG
4	6:04	CAP
6	7:56	AQU
8	12:44	PIS
10	20:31	ARI
13	6:37	TAU
15	18:15	GEM
18	6:49	CAN
20	19:21	LEO
23	6:07	VIR
25	13:22	LIB
27	16:32	SCO
29	16:39	SAG
31	15:43	CAP

JUN
2	15:59	AQU
4	19:14	PIS
7	2:11	ARI
9	12:16	TAU
12	0:11	GEM
14	12:50	CAN
17	1:19	LEO
19	12:33	VIR
21	21:04	LIB
24	1:50	SCO
26	3:09	SAG
28	2:30	CAP
30	2:00	AQU

JUL
2	1:47	PIS
4	12:54	ARI
6	1:30	TAU
9	13:39	GEM
12	0:09	CAN
14	8:31	LEO
16	14:38	VIR
18	18:35	LIB
20	20:46	SCO
22	22:07	SAG
23	23:55	CAP
28	3:39	AQU
30	10:29	PIS

AUG
3	3:46	ARI
5	9:10	TAU
8	6:10	GEM
10	7:08	CAN
13	8:08	LEO
15	9:02	VIR
17	11:58	LIB
19	12:38	SCO
21	12:37	SAG
23	13:49	CAP
25	17:55	AQU

SEP
1	20:40	GEM
4	9:00	CAN
6	21:15	LEO
9	7:31	VIR
11	15:05	LIB
13	20:19	SCO
15	23:58	SAG
18	2:48	CAP
20	5:27	AQU
22	8:34	PIS
24	12:57	ARI
26	19:34	TAU
29	5:05	GEM

OCT
1	17:03	CAN
4	5:35	LEO
6	16:13	VIR
8	23:33	LIB
11	3:46	SCO
13	6:10	SAG
15	8:13	CAP
17	11:01	AQU
19	15:05	PIS
21	20:37	ARI
24	3:52	TAU
26	13:18	GEM
29	1:00	CAN
31	13:48	LEO

NOV
3	1:19	VIR
5	9:21	LIB
7	13:27	SCO
9	14:47	SAG
11	15:18	CAP
13	16:48	AQU
15	20:29	PIS
18	2:30	ARI
20	10:38	TAU
22	20:35	GEM
25	8:17	CAN
27	21:09	LEO
30	9:29	VIR

DEC
2	18:55	LIB
5	0:06	SCO
7	1:34	SAG
9	1:07	CAP
11	0:57	AQU
13	2:56	PIS
15	8:04	ARI
17	16:16	TAU
20	2:46	GEM
22	14:46	CAN
25	3:35	LEO
27	16:10	VIR
30	2:44	LIB

—1943—

JAN
1	9:40	SCO
3	12:34	SAG
5	12:35	AQU
7	11:42	PIS
9	12:03	ARI
11	15:20	TAU
13	22:22	GEM
16	8:39	CAN
18	20:54	LEO
21	9:44	VIR
23	22:03	LIB
26	8:47	SCO
28	16:51	SAG
30	21:34	CAP

FEB
1	23:15	AQU
3	23:10	PIS
6	1:00	ARI
8	6:17	TAU
10	15:25	GEM
13	3:24	CAN
15	16:18	LEO
18	4:20	VIR
20	14:30	LIB
22	22:25	SCO
25	3:59	SAG

MAR
1	7:19	CAP
3	8:56	AQU
5	9:54	PIS
7	11:41	ARI
9	15:53	TAU
11	23:39	GEM
14	10:51	CAN
16	23:41	LEO
19	11:43	VIR
21	21:21	LIB
24	4:23	SCO
26	9:23	SAG
28	13:05	CAP
30	15:57	AQU

APR
1	18:27	PIS
3	21:17	ARI
6	1:37	TAU
8	8:41	GEM
10	19:03	CAN
13	7:39	LEO
15	19:59	VIR
18	5:41	LIB
20	12:04	SCO
22	15:56	SAG
24	18:39	CAP
26	21:21	AQU
29	0:36	PIS

MAY
1	4:39	ARI
3	9:57	TAU
5	17:16	GEM
8	3:17	CAN
10	15:39	LEO
13	4:21	VIR
15	14:44	LIB
17	21:19	SCO
20	0:39	SAG
22	2:00	CAP
24	3:23	AQU
26	5:58	PIS
28	10:16	ARI
30	16:25	TAU

JUN
2	0:29	GEM
4	10:45	CAN
6	23:03	LEO
9	12:03	VIR
11	23:22	LIB
14	6:59	SCO
16	10:36	SAG
18	11:30	CAP
20	11:33	AQU
22	12:36	PIS
24	15:52	ARI
26	21:52	TAU
29	6:27	GEM

JUL
1	17:13	CAN
4	5:39	LEO
6	18:45	VIR
9	6:44	LIB
11	15:40	SCO
13	20:37	SAG
15	21:46	CAP
17	21:46	AQU
19	23:08	PIS
22	3:53	ARI
24	12:04	TAU
26	23:04	GEM
29	11:43	CAN

AUG
3	0:45	LEO
5	12:51	VIR
7	22:40	LIB
10	5:08	SCO
12	8:09	SAG
14	8:36	CAP
16	8:06	AQU
18	8:32	PIS
20	11:39	ARI
22	18:34	TAU
25	5:07	GEM
27	17:49	CAN
30	6:47	LEO

SEP
1	18:33	VIR
4	4:20	LIB
6	11:38	SCO
8	16:13	SAG
10	18:18	CAP
12	18:46	AQU
14	19:09	PIS
16	21:14	ARI
19	2:42	TAU
21	12:10	GEM
24	0:34	CAN
26	13:30	LEO
29	0:56	VIR

OCT
1	10:04	LIB
3	17:03	SCO
5	22:11	SAG
8	1:39	CAP
10	3:44	AQU
12	5:12	PIS
14	7:26	ARI
16	12:07	TAU
18	20:29	GEM
21	8:12	CAN
23	21:10	LEO
26	8:38	VIR
28	17:14	LIB
30	23:14	SCO

NOV
2	3:37	CAP
4	7:10	AQU
6	10:16	PIS
8	13:10	ARI
10	16:32	TAU
12	21:31	GEM
15	5:22	CAN
17	16:27	LEO
20	5:21	VIR
22	17:19	LIB
25	2:09	SCO
27	7:35	SAG
29	10:43	CAP

DEC
1	13:01	AQU
3	15:36	PIS
5	19:00	ARI
7	23:30	TAU
10	5:32	GEM
12	13:46	CAN
15	0:37	LEO
17	13:22	VIR
20	1:55	LIB
22	11:46	SCO
24	17:44	SAG
26	20:24	CAP
28	21:21	AQU
30	22:17	PIS

Love Signs for Beginners

—1944—

JAN
2	0:34	ARI
4	4:58	TAU
6	11:44	GEM
8	20:48	CAN
11	7:58	LEO
13	20:38	VIR
16	9:29	LIB
18	20:28	SCO
21	3:53	SAG
23	7:27	CAP
25	8:09	AQU
27	7:48	PIS
29	8:15	ARI
31	11:07	TAU

FEB
2	17:17	GEM
5	2:40	CAN
7	14:20	LEO
10	3:08	VIR
12	15:54	LIB
15	3:24	SCO
17	12:15	SAG
19	17:33	CAP
21	19:27	AQU
23	19:09	PIS
25	18:31	ARI
27	19:36	TAU

MAR
1	0:06	GEM
3	8:38	CAN
5	20:19	LEO
8	9:18	VIR
10	21:55	LIB
13	9:12	SCO
15	18:31	SAG
18	1:13	CAP
20	4:55	AQU
22	5:59	PIS
24	5:42	ARI
26	6:01	TAU
28	8:58	GEM
30	15:59	CAN

APR
2	2:54	LEO
4	15:49	VIR
7	4:22	LIB
9	15:12	SCO
12	0:02	SAG
14	6:56	CAP
16	11:46	AQU
18	14:28	PIS
20	15:35	ARI
22	16:28	TAU
24	18:58	GEM
27	0:49	CAN
29	10:36	LEO

MAY
1	23:04	VIR
4	11:40	LIB
6	22:18	SCO
9	6:27	SAG
11	12:33	CAP
13	17:10	AQU
15	20:35	PIS
17	23:03	ARI
20	1:15	TAU
22	4:26	GEM
24	10:04	CAN
26	19:04	LEO
29	6:58	VIR
31	19:37	LIB

JUN
3	6:32	SCO
5	14:27	SAG
7	19:41	CAP
9	23:12	AQU
12	1:58	PIS
14	4:41	ARI
16	7:52	TAU
18	12:11	GEM
20	18:28	CAN
23	3:25	LEO
25	14:58	VIR
28	3:40	LIB
30	15:10	SCO

JUL
2	23:38	SAG
5	4:42	CAP
7	7:14	AQU
9	8:39	PIS
11	10:18	ARI
13	13:16	TAU
15	18:11	GEM
18	1:21	CAN
20	10:51	LEO
22	22:24	VIR
25	11:08	LIB
27	23:16	SCO
30	8:50	SAG

AUG
1	14:42	CAP
3	17:10	AQU
5	17:35	PIS
7	17:43	ARI
9	19:19	TAU
11	23:38	GEM
14	7:03	CAN
16	17:08	LEO
19	5:01	VIR
21	17:45	LIB
24	6:13	SCO
26	16:52	SAG
29	0:12	CAP
31	3:44	AQU

SEP
2	4:14	PIS
4	3:27	ARI
6	3:28	TAU
8	6:13	GEM
10	12:47	CAN
12	22:50	LEO
15	11:00	VIR
17	23:48	LIB
20	12:11	SCO
22	23:16	SAG
25	7:55	CAP
27	13:10	AQU
29	14:58	PIS

OCT
1	14:30	ARI
3	13:46	TAU
5	14:59	GEM
7	19:56	CAN
10	5:03	LEO
12	17:04	VIR
15	5:55	LIB
17	18:03	SCO
20	4:50	SAG
22	13:48	CAP
24	20:19	AQU
26	23:53	PIS
29	0:54	ARI
31	0:45	TAU

NOV
2	1:28	GEM
4	5:04	CAN
6	12:44	LEO
9	0:00	VIR
11	12:45	LIB
14	1:02	SCO
16	11:39	SAG
18	20:01	CAP
21	1:47	AQU
23	6:18	PIS
25	8:57	ARI
27	10:22	TAU
29	11:55	GEM

DEC
1	15:16	CAN
3	21:53	LEO
6	8:04	VIR
8	20:29	LIB
11	8:42	SCO
13	18:50	SAG
16	2:22	CAP
18	7:44	AQU
20	11:39	PIS
22	14:42	ARI
24	17:24	TAU
26	20:26	GEM
29	0:44	CAN
31	7:19	LEO

—1945—

JAN
2	16:49	VIR
5	4:44	LIB
7	17:13	SCO
10	3:55	SAG
12	11:28	CAP
14	15:57	AQU
16	18:27	PIS
18	20:21	ARI
20	22:48	TAU
23	2:35	GEM
25	8:05	CAN
27	15:33	LEO
30	1:09	VIR

FEB
1	12:46	LIB
4	1:22	SCO
6	12:57	SAG
8	21:29	CAP
11	2:12	AQU
13	3:52	PIS
15	4:12	ARI
17	5:05	TAU
19	8:01	GEM
21	13:42	CAN
23	21:58	LEO
26	8:13	VIR
28	19:57	LIB

MAR
3	8:32	SCO
5	20:45	SAG
8	6:37	CAP
10	12:40	AQU
12	14:50	PIS
14	14:32	ARI
16	15:04	TAU
18	15:31	GEM
20	19:31	CAN
23	3:32	LEO
25	14:11	VIR
28	2:15	LIB
30	14:50	SCO

APR
2	3:08	SAG
4	13:51	CAP
6	21:28	AQU
9	1:10	PIS
11	1:38	ARI
13	0:40	TAU
15	0:31	GEM
17	3:13	CAN
19	9:52	LEO
21	20:03	VIR
24	8:15	LIB
26	20:52	SCO
29	8:56	SAG

MAY
1	19:40	CAP
4	4:06	AQU
6	9:21	PIS
8	11:25	ARI
10	11:24	TAU
12	11:12	GEM
14	12:51	CAN
16	17:57	LEO
19	2:35	VIR
21	14:43	LIB
24	3:21	SCO
26	15:11	SAG
29	1:24	CAP
31	9:35	AQU

JUN
2	15:25	PIS
4	18:51	ARI
6	20:23	TAU
8	21:15	GEM
10	23:02	CAN
13	3:20	LEO
15	11:07	VIR
17	22:06	LIB
20	10:36	SCO
22	22:27	SAG
25	8:14	CAP
27	15:36	AQU
29	20:51	PIS

JUL
2	0:29	ARI
4	3:04	TAU
6	5:20	GEM
8	8:10	CAN
10	12:43	LEO
12	19:58	VIR
15	6:13	LIB
17	18:29	SCO
20	6:36	SAG
22	16:29	CAP
24	23:27	AQU
27	3:27	PIS
29	6:07	ARI
31	8:29	TAU

AUG
2	11:23	GEM
4	15:23	CAN
6	20:53	LEO
9	4:24	VIR
11	14:21	LIB
14	2:24	SCO
16	14:56	SAG
19	1:31	CAP
21	8:32	AQU
23	12:05	PIS
25	13:30	ARI
27	14:23	TAU
29	16:47	GEM
31	21:00	CAN

SEP
3	3:20	LEO
5	11:36	VIR
7	21:48	LIB
10	9:48	SCO
12	22:37	SAG
15	10:11	CAP
17	18:20	AQU
19	22:19	PIS
21	23:11	ARI
23	22:53	TAU
25	23:32	GEM
28	2:38	CAN
30	8:47	LEO

OCT
2	17:34	VIR
5	4:17	LIB
7	16:24	SCO
10	5:17	SAG
12	17:33	CAP
15	3:07	AQU
17	8:34	PIS
19	10:09	ARI
21	9:30	TAU
23	8:49	GEM
25	10:11	CAN
27	14:55	LEO
29	23:12	VIR

NOV
1	10:08	LIB
3	22:29	SCO
6	11:18	SAG
8	23:35	CAP
11	9:59	AQU
13	17:05	PIS
15	20:24	ARI
17	20:48	TAU
19	20:02	GEM
21	20:14	CAN
23	23:12	LEO
26	5:59	VIR
28	16:18	LIB

DEC
1	4:43	SCO
3	17:30	SAG
6	5:23	CAP
8	15:34	AQU
10	23:20	PIS
13	4:15	ARI
15	6:30	TAU
17	7:03	GEM
19	7:27	CAN
21	9:30	LEO
23	14:44	VIR
25	23:45	LIB
28	11:43	SCO
31	0:32	SAG

—1946—

JAN
2	12:11	CAP
4	21:38	AQU
7	4:47	PIS
9	9:56	ARI
11	13:25	TAU
13	15:42	GEM
15	17:32	CAN
17	20:03	LEO
20	0:40	VIR
22	8:31	LIB
24	19:40	SCO
27	8:27	SAG
29	20:18	CAP

FEB
1	5:24	AQU
3	11:32	PIS
5	15:38	ARI
7	18:47	TAU
9	21:45	GEM
12	0:59	CAN
14	4:50	LEO
16	10:03	VIR
18	17:36	LIB
21	4:05	SCO
23	16:41	SAG
26	5:01	CAP
28	14:34	AQU

MAR
2	20:25	PIS
4	23:23	ARI
7	1:08	TAU
9	3:12	GEM
11	6:29	CAN
13	11:14	LEO
15	17:32	VIR
18	1:40	LIB
20	12:04	SCO
23	0:30	SAG
25	13:18	CAP
27	23:51	AQU
30	6:26	PIS

APR
1	9:16	ARI
3	9:56	TAU
5	10:25	GEM
7	12:37	CAN
9	16:37	LEO
11	23:20	VIR
14	8:13	LIB
16	19:03	SCO
19	7:30	SAG
21	20:28	CAP
24	7:56	AQU
26	15:54	PIS
28	19:45	ARI
30	20:31	TAU

MAY
2	20:23	GEM
4	20:23	CAN
6	23:04	LEO
9	4:57	VIR
11	13:53	LIB
14	1:08	SCO
16	13:46	SAG
19	2:42	CAP
21	14:31	AQU
23	23:38	PIS
26	5:05	ARI
28	7:04	TAU
30	6:54	GEM

JUN
1	6:28	CAN
3	7:39	LEO
5	11:57	VIR
7	19:57	LIB
10	7:04	SCO
12	19:50	SAG
15	8:39	CAP
17	20:16	AQU
20	5:43	PIS
22	12:19	ARI
24	15:56	TAU
26	17:07	GEM
28	17:10	CAN
30	17:47	LEO

JUL
2	20:45	VIR
5	3:21	LIB
7	13:41	SCO
10	2:20	SAG
12	15:05	CAP
15	2:17	AQU
17	11:15	PIS
19	17:59	ARI
21	22:35	TAU
24	1:18	GEM
26	2:44	CAN
28	3:57	LEO
30	6:32	VIR

AUG
1	12:05	LIB
3	21:23	SCO
6	9:36	SAG
8	22:23	CAP
11	9:24	AQU
13	17:41	PIS
15	23:37	ARI
18	3:59	TAU
20	7:22	GEM
22	10:06	CAN
24	12:38	LEO
26	15:54	VIR
28	21:15	LIB
31	5:49	SCO

SEP
2	17:31	SAG
5	6:24	CAP
7	17:41	AQU
10	1:46	PIS
12	6:49	ARI
14	10:03	TAU
16	12:45	GEM
18	15:42	CAN
20	19:13	LEO
22	23:38	VIR
25	5:40	LIV
27	14:12	SCO
30	1:32	SAG

OCT
2	14:29	CAP
5	2:27	AQU
7	11:09	PIS
9	16:20	ARI
11	19:37	TAU
13	21:23	GEM
16	0:35	CAN
18	5:35	LEO
20	12:33	VIR
22	21:41	LIB
25	9:03	SCO
27	21:59	CAP

NOV
1	10:36	AQU
3	20:32	PIS
6	2:28	ARI
8	4:49	TAU
10	5:07	GEM
12	5:15	CAN
14	6:53	LEO
16	11:05	VIR
18	18:12	LIB
21	3:58	SCO
23	15:44	SAG
26	4:40	CAP
28	17:30	AQU

DEC
1	4:30	PIS
3	12:05	ARI
5	15:48	TAU
7	16:30	GEM
9	15:46	CAN
11	15:50	LEO
13	18:09	VIR
16	0:07	LIB
18	9:43	SCO
20	21:48	SAG
23	10:50	CAP
25	23:29	AQU
28	10:43	PIS
30	19:31	ARI

—1947—

JAN
2	1:06	TAU
4	3:26	GEM
6	3:28	CAN
8	2:53	LEO
10	3:44	VIR
12	16:15	LIB
14	12:41	SCO
17	4:03	SAG
19	16:15	CAP
22	17:10	AQU
24	5:37	PIS
27	16:23	ARI
29	1:10	TAU
31	7:45	GEM
	11:52	

FEB
2	13:38	CAN
4	14:01	LEO
6	14:42	VIR
8	17:39	LIB
11	0:28	SCO
13	11:14	SAG
16	0:12	CAP
18	12:39	AQU
20	22:57	PIS
23	6:58	ARI
25	13:08	TAU
27	17:47	GEM

MAR
1	20:59	CAN
3	23:00	LEO
6	0:46	VIR
8	3:51	LIB
10	9:51	SCO
12	19:34	SAG
15	8:00	CAP
17	20:35	AQU
20	6:57	PIS
22	14:23	ARI
24	19:29	TAU
26	23:16	GEM
29	2:26	CAN
31	5:22	LEO

APR
2	8:30	VIR
4	12:39	LIB
6	18:56	SCO
9	4:12	SAG
11	16:08	CAP
14	4:51	AQU
16	15:47	PIS
18	23:26	ARI
21	3:56	TAU
23	6:27	GEM
25	8:22	CAN
27	10:44	LEO
29	14:15	VIR

MAY
1	19:24	LIB
4	2:35	SCO
6	12:09	SAG
8	23:55	CAP
11	12:41	AQU
14	0:20	PIS
16	8:56	ARI
18	13:51	TAU
20	15:51	GEM
22	16:27	CAN
24	17:18	LEO
26	19:50	VIR
29	0:54	LIB
31	8:42	SCO

JUN
2	18:54	SAG
5	6:51	CAP
7	19:38	AQU
10	7:47	PIS
12	17:34	ARI
14	23:45	TAU
17	2:22	GEM
19	2:32	CAN
21	2:06	LEO
23	3:01	VIR
25	6:51	LIB
27	14:17	SCO
30	0:46	SAG

JUL
2	13:03	CAP
5	1:50	AQU
7	14:03	PIS
10	0:34	ARI
12	8:12	TAU
14	12:17	GEM
16	13:14	CAN
18	12:34	LEO
20	12:19	VIR
22	14:33	LIB
24	20:41	SCO
27	6:40	SAG
29	19:01	CAP

AUG
1	7:50	AQU
3	19:39	PIS
6	6:20	ARI
8	14:43	TAU
10	20:17	GEM
12	22:49	CAN
14	23:06	LEO
16	22:49	VIR
19	0:04	LIB
21	4:44	SCO
23	13:34	SAG
26	1:31	CAP
28	14:18	AQU
31	2:03	PIS

SEP
2	12:03	ARI
4	20:10	TAU
7	2:18	GEM
9	6:12	CAN
11	8:51	LEO
13	10:16	VIR
15	14:10	LIB
17	21:49	SCO
19	8:58	SAG
22	21:38	CAP
25	9:24	AQU
29	18:58	ARI

OCT
2	2:15	TAU
4	7:44	GEM
6	11:47	CAN
8	14:41	LEO
10	16:57	VIR
12	19:31	LIB
15	23:45	SCO
17	17:14	SAG
19	17:46	CAP
22	5:39	AQU
25	3:31	PIS
27	10:16	ARI
31	14:36	GEM

NOV
2	17:32	CAN
4	20:03	LEO
6	22:55	VIR
9	2:42	LIB
11	8:02	SCO
13	15:33	SAG
16	1:37	CAP
18	13:45	AQU
21	2:16	PIS
23	12:53	ARI
26	20:06	TAU
28	23:55	GEM
30	1:31	CAN

DEC
2	2:30	LEO
4	4:23	VIR
6	8:14	LIB
8	14:24	SCO
10	22:49	SAG
13	9:14	CAP
15	21:16	AQU
18	9:59	PIS
20	21:37	ARI
23	6:11	TAU
25	10:47	GEM
27	12:03	CAN
29	11:41	LEO
31	11:47	VIR

— 99 —

LOVE SIGNS FOR BEGINNERS

—1948—

JAN
2	14:10	LIB
4	19:51	SCO
6	18:34	SAG
9	15:41	CAP
12	3:54	AQU
14	16:35	PIS
17	4:44	ARI
19	14:42	TAU
21	21:01	GEM
23	23:23	CAN
25	23:00	LEO
27	21:56	VIR
29	22:29	LIB

FEB
1	2:27	SCO
3	10:26	SAG
5	21:30	CAP
8	9:59	AQU
10	22:37	PIS
13	10:37	ARI
15	21:08	TAU
18	4:56	GEM
20	9:09	CAN
22	10:07	LEO
24	9:22	VIR
26	9:05	LIB
28	11:24	SCO

MAR
1	17:41	SAG
4	3:50	CAP
6	16:14	AQU
9	4:53	PIS
11	16:33	ARI
14	2:40	TAU
16	10:45	GEM
18	16:14	CAN
20	18:58	LEO
22	19:42	VIR
24	20:01	LIB
26	21:49	SCO
29	2:46	SAG
31	11:34	CAP

APR
2	23:18	AQU
5	11:56	PIS
7	23:28	ARI
10	8:58	TAU
12	16:20	GEM
14	21:41	CAN
17	1:16	LEO
19	3:30	VIR
21	5:16	LIB
23	7:49	SCO
25	12:31	SAG
27	20:22	CAP
30	7:16	AQU

MAY
2	19:44	PIS
5	7:28	ARI
7	16:48	TAU
9	23:20	GEM
12	3:38	CAN
14	6:39	LEO
16	9:14	VIR
18	12:07	LIB
20	15:56	SCO
22	21:22	SAG
25	5:08	CAP
27	15:31	AQU
30	3:46	PIS

JUN
1	15:55	ARI
4	1:43	TAU
6	8:06	GEM
8	11:28	CAN
10	13:11	LEO
12	14:49	VIR
14	17:33	LIB
16	22:03	SCO
19	4:28	SAG
21	12:51	CAP
23	23:15	AQU
26	11:23	PIS
28	23:56	ARI

JUL
1	10:40	TAU
3	17:48	GEM
5	21:07	CAN
7	21:53	LEO
9	22:03	VIR
11	23:31	LIB
14	3:28	SCO
16	10:11	SAG
18	19:13	CAP
21	6:02	AQU
23	18:13	PIS
26	6:57	ARI
28	18:34	TAU
31	3:01	GEM

AUG
2	7:20	CAN
4	8:13	LEO
6	7:32	VIR
8	7:29	LIB
10	9:56	SCO
12	15:49	SAG
15	0:51	CAP
17	12:03	AQU
20	0:23	PIS
22	13:05	ARI
25	1:03	TAU
27	10:40	GEM
29	16:34	CAN
31	18:41	LEO

SEP
2	18:20	VIR
4	17:35	LIB
6	18:34	SCO
8	22:52	SAG
11	6:56	CAP
13	17:58	AQU
16	6:27	PIS
18	19:02	ARI
21	6:45	TAU
23	16:40	GEM
25	23:46	CAN
28	3:35	LEO
30	4:40	VIR

OCT
2	4:30	LIB
4	4:58	SCO
6	7:55	SAG
8	14:31	CAP
11	0:42	AQU
13	13:03	PIS
16	1:36	ARI
18	12:54	TAU
20	22:15	GEM
23	5:21	CAN
25	10:10	LEO
27	12:53	VIR
29	14:16	LIB
31	15:31	SCO

NOV
2	18:10	SAG
4	23:39	CAP
7	8:41	AQU
9	20:34	PIS
12	9:12	ARI
14	20:24	TAU
17	5:02	GEM
19	11:11	CAN
21	15:32	LEO
23	18:48	VIR
25	21:33	LIB
28	0:19	SCO
30	3:52	SAG

DEC
2	9:16	CAP
4	17:32	AQU
7	4:46	PIS
9	17:30	ARI
12	5:09	TAU
14	13:44	GEM
16	19:01	CAN
18	22:03	LEO
21	0:19	VIR
23	2:59	LIB
25	6:39	SCO
27	11:29	SAG
29	17:47	CAP

—1949—

JAN
3	2:07	AQU
5	12:58	PIS
8	1:40	ARI
10	14:03	TAU
13	23:31	GEM
15	4:57	CAN
17	7:08	LEO
19	7:52	VIR
21	9:03	LIB
23	11:59	SCO
25	17:09	SAG
28	0:22	CAP
30	9:26	AQU
30	20:26	PIS

FEB
2	9:04	ARI
4	21:57	TAU
7	8:40	GEM
9	15:22	CAN
11	18:01	LEO
13	18:05	VIR
15	17:44	LIB
17	18:53	SCO
19	22:49	SAG
22	5:50	CAP
24	15:26	AQU
27	2:54	PIS

MAR
1	15:36	ARI
4	4:33	TAU
6	16:05	GEM
9	0:21	CAN
11	4:33	LEO
13	5:24	VIR
15	4:40	LIB
17	4:25	SCO
19	6:30	SAG
21	12:04	CAP
23	21:10	AQU
26	8:50	PIS
28	21:41	ARI
31	10:29	TAU

APR
2	22:03	GEM
5	7:10	CAN
7	12:59	LEO
9	15:48	VIR
11	15:27	LIB
13	15:48	SCO
15	16:23	SAG
17	20:16	CAP
20	3:59	AQU
22	15:08	PIS
25	4:01	ARI
27	16:41	TAU
30	3:48	GEM

MAY
2	12:43	CAN
4	19:11	LEO
6	23:11	VIR
9	1:07	LIB
11	1:54	SCO
13	2:57	SAG
15	5:57	CAP
17	12:19	AQU
19	22:26	PIS
22	11:02	ARI
24	23:42	TAU
27	10:27	GEM
29	18:39	CAN

JUN
1	0:36	LEO
3	4:53	VIR
5	7:58	LIB
7	10:13	SCO
9	12:24	SAG
11	15:01	CAP
13	21:26	AQU
16	6:38	PIS
18	18:45	ARI
21	7:30	TAU
23	18:20	GEM
26	2:01	CAN
28	6:58	LEO
30	10:27	VIR

JUL
2	13:22	LIB
4	16:22	SCO
6	19:45	SAG
9	0:02	CAP
11	6:09	AQU
13	15:01	PIS
16	2:43	ARI
18	15:36	TAU
21	2:57	GEM
23	10:52	CAN
25	15:19	LEO
27	17:36	VIR
29	19:20	LIB
31	21:44	SCO

AUG
3	1:25	SAG
5	6:36	CAP
7	13:34	AQU
9	22:45	PIS
12	10:20	ARI
14	23:18	TAU
17	11:23	GEM
19	20:15	CAN
22	1:08	LEO
24	2:56	VIR
26	3:24	LIB
28	4:19	SCO
30	7:00	SAG

SEP
1	12:05	CAP
3	19:37	AQU
6	5:26	PIS
8	17:13	ARI
11	6:12	TAU
13	18:47	GEM
16	4:52	CAN
18	11:05	LEO
20	13:34	VIR
22	13:42	LIB
24	13:20	SCO
26	14:21	SAG
28	18:07	CAP

OCT
1	1:13	AQU
3	11:20	PIS
5	23:27	ARI
8	12:26	TAU
11	1:02	GEM
13	11:51	CAN
15	19:35	LEO
17	23:42	VIR
20	0:48	LIB
22	0:18	SCO
24	0:08	SAG
26	2:10	CAP
28	7:50	AQU
30	17:21	PIS

NOV
2	5:34	ARI
4	18:37	TAU
7	6:55	GEM
9	17:35	CAN
12	2:00	LEO
14	7:42	VIR
16	10:36	LIB
18	11:18	SCO
20	11:15	SAG
22	12:19	CAP
24	16:24	AQU
27	0:35	PIS
29	12:18	ARI

DEC
2	1:22	TAU
4	13:28	GEM
6	23:31	CAN
9	7:27	LEO
11	13:31	VIR
13	17:45	LIB
15	20:13	SCO
17	21:32	SAG
19	23:00	CAP
22	2:24	AQU
24	9:20	PIS
26	20:05	ARI
29	8:58	TAU
31	21:13	GEM

— 100 —

—1950—

JAN			FEB			MAR			APR		
3	6:56	CAN	1	22:34	CAN	1	8:30	LEO	2	0:41	LIB
5	13:58	LEO	4	2:37	LEO	3	12:24	VIR	4	0:35	SCO
7	19:06	VIR	6	5:19	VIR	5	14:00	LIB	6	0:37	SAG
9	23:08	LIB	8	7:50	LIB	7	14:55	SCO	8	2:29	CAP
12	2:28	SCO	10	10:51	SCO	9	16:37	SAG	10	7:24	AQU
14	5:16	SAG	12	14:45	SAG	11	20:07	CAP	12	15:38	PIS
16	8:06	CAP	14	19:57	CAP	14	1:52	AQU	15	2:32	ARI
18	12:07	AQU	17	3:11	AQU	16	9:59	PIS	17	15:00	TAU
20	18:41	PIS	19	13:01	PIS	18	20:21	ARI	20	3:54	GEM
23	4:37	ARI	22	1:12	ARI	21	8:32	TAU	22	16:02	CAN
25	17:08	TAU	24	14:03	TAU	23	21:28	GEM	25	1:57	LEO
28	5:43	GEM	27	1:03	GEM	26	9:17	CAN	27	8:30	VIR
30	15:50	CAN				28	18:05	LEO	29	11:25	LIB
						30	23:01	VIR			

MAY			JUN			JUL			AUG		
1	11:37	SCO	3	21:27	CAP	1	9:19	AQU	2	7:03	ARI
3	10:50	SAG	5	23:18	AQU	3	13:51	PIS	4	18:06	TAU
5	11:08	CAP	8	4:57	PIS	5	22:24	ARI	7	6:44	GEM
7	14:22	AQU	10	14:44	ARI	8	10:13	TAU	9	18:27	CAN
9	21:34	PIS	13	3:12	TAU	10	23:02	GEM	12	3:36	LEO
12	8:18	ARI	15	16:05	GEM	13	10:34	CAN	14	10:03	VIR
14	20:59	TAU	18	3:45	CAN	15	19:52	LEO	16	14:31	LIB
17	9:52	GEM	20	13:37	LEO	18	3:05	VIR	18	17:49	SCO
19	21:50	CAN	22	21:31	VIR	20	8:34	LIB	20	20:36	SAG
22	8:06	LEO	25	3:09	LIB	22	12:27	SCO	22	23:23	CAP
24	15:51	VIR	27	6:19	SCO	24	14:55	SAG	25	2:53	AQU
26	20:26	LIB	29	7:26	SAG	26	16:39	CAP	27	8:02	PIS
28	22:01	SCO				28	18:55	AQU	29	15:44	ARI
30	21:43	SAG				30	23:19	PIS			

SEP			OCT			NOV			DEC		
1	2:19	TAU	3	10:59	CAN	2	10:40	VIR	1	21:53	VIR
3	14:45	GEM	5	21:40	LEO	4	16:54	LIB	4	4:29	LIB
6	2:54	CAN	8	4:54	VIR	6	19:10	SCO	6	7:19	SCO
8	12:34	LEO	10	8:29	LIB	8	20:29	SAG	8	7:17	SAG
10	18:55	VIR	12	9:31	SCO	10	19:51	CAP	10	6:16	CAP
12	22:28	LIB	14	9:44	SAG	12	19:25	AQU	12	6:34	AQU
15	0:27	SCO	16	10:55	CAP	15	21:14	PIS	14	10:10	PIS
17	2:12	SAG	18	14:27	AQU	17	2:38	ARI	16	17:58	ARI
19	4:49	CAP	20	20:53	PIS	19	11:39	TAU	19	5:10	TAU
21	8:59	AQU	23	5:59	ARI	21	23:08	GEM	21	17:49	GEM
23	15:09	PIS	25	17:03	TAU	24	11:38	CAN	24	6:18	CAN
25	23:32	ARI	28	5:22	GEM	27	0:13	LEO	26	17:45	LEO
28	10:08	TAU	30	18:03	CAN	29	12:02	VIR	29	3:41	VIR
30	22:26	GEM							31	11:20	LIB

—1951—

JAN			FEB			MAR			APR		
2	15:58	SCO	1	1:16	SAG	2	9:29	CAP	2	22:45	PIS
4	17:38	SAG	3	2:52	CAP	4	12:11	AQU	5	5:16	ARI
6	17:32	CAP	5	4:04	AQU	6	15:45	PIS	7	13:52	TAU
8	17:35	AQU	7	6:29	PIS	8	21:16	ARI	10	0:41	GEM
10	19:56	PIS	9	11:43	ARI	11	5:33	TAU	12	13:04	CAN
13	2:05	ARI	11	20:33	TAU	13	16:36	GEM	15	1:18	LEO
15	12:10	TAU	14	8:18	GEM	16	5:06	CAN	17	11:07	VIR
18	0:36	GEM	16	20:51	CAN	18	16:44	LEO	19	17:13	LIB
20	13:06	CAN	19	8:01	LEO	21	1:39	VIR	21	19:55	SCO
23	0:12	LEO	21	16:43	VIR	23	7:21	LIB	23	20:40	SAG
25	9:26	VIR	23	23:01	LIB	25	10:36	SCO	25	21:19	CAP
27	16:46	LIB	26	3:31	SCO	27	12:40	SAG	27	23:32	AQU
29	22:04	SCO	28	6:49	SAG	29	14:51	CAP	30	4:13	PIS
						31	18:02	AQU			

MAY			JUN			JUL			AUG		
2	11:26	ARI	1	2:33	TAU	3	8:27	CAN	2	3:08	VIR
4	20:47	TAU	3	14:03	GEM	5	21:00	LEO	4	14:18	LIB
7	7:51	GEM	6	2:31	CAN	8	8:36	VIR	6	23:34	SCO
9	20:13	CAN	8	15:12	LEO	10	18:04	LIB	9	6:24	SAG
12	8:49	LEO	11	2:47	VIR	13	0:19	SCO	11	10:31	CAP
14	19:44	VIR	13	11:31	LIB	15	3:03	SAG	13	12:18	AQU
17	3:05	LIB	15	16:17	SCO	17	3:14	CAP	15	12:53	PIS
19	6:23	SCO	17	17:26	SAG	19	2:41	AQU	17	13:52	ARI
21	6:44	SAG	19	16:38	CAP	21	3:28	PIS	19	16:58	TAU
23	6:07	CAP	21	16:04	AQU	23	7:21	ARI	21	23:26	GEM
25	6:41	AQU	23	17:49	PIS	25	15:07	TAU	24	9:27	CAN
27	10:05	PIS	25	23:13	ARI	28	2:08	GEM	26	21:44	LEO
29	16:53	ARI	28	8:17	TAU	30	14:42	CAN	29	10:10	VIR
			30	19:51	GEM				31	21:00	LIB

SEP			OCT			NOV			DEC		
3	5:32	SCO	2	18:23	SAG	1	5:20	CAP	2	15:45	PIS
5	11:49	SAG	4	21:48	CAP	3	6:40	AQU	4	18:08	ARI
7	16:11	CAP	7	0:30	AQU	5	8:43	PIS	6	23:18	TAU
9	19:06	AQU	9	3:19	PIS	7	12:23	ARI	9	7:04	GEM
11	21:11	PIS	11	6:46	ARI	9	17:53	TAU	11	16:54	CAN
13	23:21	ARI	13	11:19	TAU	12	1:07	GEM	14	4:22	LEO
16	2:47	TAU	15	17:37	GEM	14	10:15	CAN	16	17:05	VIR
18	8:41	GEM	18	2:22	CAN	16	21:27	LEO	19	5:52	LIB
20	17:47	CAN	20	13:42	LEO	19	10:12	VIR	21	16:41	SCO
23	5:34	LEO	23	2:25	VIR	21	22:36	LIB	23	23:39	SAG
25	18:08	VIR	25	14:01	LIB	24	8:09	SCO	26	2:27	CAP
28	5:08	LIB	27	22:25	SCO	26	13:32	SAG	28	2:24	AQU
30	13:08	SCO	30	3:09	SAG	28	15:20	CAP	30	1:36	PIS
						30	15:22	AQU			

— 101 —

LOVE SIGNS FOR BEGINNERS

—1952—

JAN
1	AQU	2:10	PIS
3	PIS	5:42	ARI
5	ARI	8:57	TAU
8	TAU	12:43	GEM
10	GEM	10:48	CAN
12	CAN	16:06	LEO
14	LEO	23:19	VIR
17	VIR	1:24	LIB
19	LIB	13:38	SCO
22	SCO	2:42	SAG
24	SAG	14:41	CAP
26	CAP	0:43	AQU
29	AQU	8:33	PIS
31	PIS	14:06	ARI

FEB
2	ARI	17:24	TAU
4	TAU	19:51	GEM
6	GEM	4:55	CAN
8	CAN	16:44	LEO
11	LEO	5:36	VIR
13	VIR	18:02	LIB
16	LIB	5:00	SCO
18	SCO	13:45	SAG
20	SAG	19:42	CAP
22	CAP	22:49	AQU
24	AQU	23:48	PIS
27	PIS	0:01	ARI
29	ARI	1:11	TAU

MAR
2	TAU	12:36	GEM
4	GEM	12:30	CAN
7	CAN	12:30	LEO
10	LEO	11:16	VIR
12	VIR	19:20	LIB
15	LIB	1:15	SCO
17	SCO	5:19	SAG
19	SAG	9:39	CAP
22	CAP	11:34	AQU
24	AQU	15:05	PIS
26	PIS	21:36	ARI
29	ARI	—	TAU

APR
1	TAU	7:39	GEM
3	GEM	20:10	CAN
6	CAN	8:40	LEO
8	LEO	18:56	VIR
11	VIR	2:13	LIB
13	LIB	7:08	SCO
15	SCO	10:41	SAG
17	SAG	13:43	CAP
19	CAP	16:56	AQU
21	AQU	19:56	PIS
24	PIS	0:15	ARI
26	ARI	6:40	TAU
28	TAU	16:06	GEM

MAY
1	GEM	4:12	CAN
3	CAN	16:57	LEO
6	LEO	3:39	VIR
8	VIR	10:49	LIB
10	LIB	14:50	SCO
12	SCO	17:09	SAG
14	SAG	19:14	CAP
16	CAP	22:05	AQU
19	AQU	2:07	PIS
21	PIS	7:29	ARI
23	ARI	14:37	TAU
26	TAU	0:06	GEM
28	GEM	11:59	CAN
31	CAN	0:57	LEO

JUN
2	LEO	12:26	VIR
4	VIR	20:19	LIB
7	LIB	0:21	SCO
9	SCO	1:46	SAG
11	SAG	2:26	CAP
13	CAP	4:00	AQU
15	AQU	7:29	PIS
17	PIS	13:11	ARI
19	ARI	21:03	TAU
22	TAU	7:04	GEM
24	GEM	19:02	CAN
27	CAN	8:06	LEO
29	LEO	20:18	VIR

JUL
2	VIR	5:25	LIB
4	LIB	10:27	SCO
6	SCO	12:02	SAG
8	SAG	11:59	CAP
10	CAP	11:56	AQU
12	AQU	13:56	PIS
14	PIS	18:45	ARI
17	ARI	2:37	TAU
19	TAU	13:05	GEM
22	GEM	1:20	CAN
24	CAN	14:25	LEO
27	LEO	2:54	VIR
29	VIR	13:04	LIB
31	LIB	19:37	SCO

AUG
2	SCO	22:41	SAG
4	SAG	22:41	CAP
6	CAP	22:05	AQU
8	AQU	22:33	PIS
11	PIS	1:46	ARI
13	ARI	8:36	TAU
15	TAU	18:52	GEM
18	GEM	7:19	CAN
20	CAN	20:22	LEO
23	LEO	8:42	VIR
25	VIR	19:10	LIB
28	LIB	2:53	SCO
30	SCO	7:24	SAG

SEP
1	SAG	9:03	CAP
3	CAP	9:00	AQU
5	AQU	8:57	PIS
7	PIS	10:48	ARI
9	ARI	16:06	TAU
12	TAU	1:24	GEM
14	GEM	13:38	CAN
17	CAN	2:42	LEO
19	LEO	14:41	VIR
22	VIR	0:43	LIB
24	LIB	8:33	SCO
26	SCO	14:06	SAG
28	SAG	17:24	CAP
30	CAP	18:52	AQU

OCT
2	AQU	19:34	PIS
4	PIS	21:05	ARI
7	ARI	1:15	TAU
9	TAU	9:16	GEM
11	GEM	20:50	CAN
14	CAN	9:51	LEO
16	LEO	21:44	VIR
19	VIR	7:10	LIB
21	LIB	14:12	SCO
23	SCO	19:28	SAG
25	SAG	23:28	CAP
28	CAP	2:23	AQU
30	AQU	4:34	PIS

NOV
1	PIS	6:58	TAU
3	TAU	11:02	GEM
5	GEM	18:12	CAN
8	CAN	4:56	LEO
10	LEO	17:47	VIR
13	VIR	5:18	LIB
15	LIB	15:18	SCO
17	SCO	21:33	SAG
20	SAG	1:40	CAP
22	CAP	4:52	AQU
24	AQU	7:55	PIS
26	PIS	11:09	ARI
28	ARI	14:54	TAU
30	TAU	19:53	GEM

DEC
3	GEM	3:09	CAN
5	CAN	13:23	LEO
8	LEO	1:57	VIR
10	VIR	14:35	LIB
13	LIB	0:39	SCO
15	SCO	7:00	SAG
17	SAG	10:17	CAP
19	CAP	12:02	AQU
21	AQU	13:45	PIS
23	PIS	16:30	ARI
25	ARI	20:46	TAU
28	TAU	2:48	GEM
30	GEM	10:53	CAN

—1953—

JAN
1	CAN	21:7	LEO
4	LEO	9:41	VIR
6	VIR	22:36	LIB
9	LIB	9:44	SCO
11	SCO	17:14	SAG
13	SAG	20:55	CAP
15	CAP	21:57	AQU
17	AQU	22:07	PIS
19	PIS	23:08	ARI
22	ARI	2:20	TAU
24	TAU	8:21	GEM
26	GEM	17:07	CAN
29	CAN	4:06	LEO
31	LEO	16:35	VIR

FEB
3	VIR	5:31	LIB
5	LIB	17:21	SCO
8	SCO	2:20	SAG
10	SAG	7:32	CAP
12	CAP	9:17	AQU
14	AQU	8:58	PIS
16	PIS	8:30	ARI
18	ARI	9:50	TAU
20	TAU	14:27	GEM
22	GEM	22:48	CAN
25	CAN	10:05	LEO
27	LEO	22:51	VIR

MAR
2	VIR	11:41	LIB
4	LIB	23:31	SCO
7	SCO	9:20	SAG
9	SAG	16:10	CAP
11	CAP	20:17	AQU
13	AQU	19:37	PIS
15	PIS	19:39	ARI
17	ARI	19:44	TAU
19	TAU	22:35	GEM
22	GEM	5:29	CAN
24	CAN	16:14	LEO
27	LEO	5:04	VIR
29	VIR	17:51	LIB

APR
1	LIB	5:19	SCO
3	SCO	14:58	SAG
5	SAG	22:29	CAP
8	CAP	3:27	AQU
10	AQU	5:49	PIS
12	PIS	6:19	ARI
14	ARI	6:31	TAU
16	TAU	8:27	GEM
18	GEM	13:53	CAN
20	CAN	23:27	LEO
23	LEO	11:53	VIR
26	VIR	0:40	LIB
28	LIB	11:52	SCO
30	SCO	20:52	SAG

MAY
3	SAG	3:55	CAP
5	CAP	9:12	AQU
7	AQU	12:46	PIS
9	PIS	14:49	ARI
11	ARI	16:12	TAU
13	TAU	18:27	GEM
15	GEM	23:16	CAN
18	CAN	7:47	LEO
20	LEO	19:31	VIR
23	VIR	8:16	LIB
25	LIB	19:32	SCO
28	SCO	4:08	SAG
30	SAG	10:17	CAP

JUN
1	CAP	14:45	AQU
3	AQU	18:12	PIS
5	PIS	21:01	ARI
7	ARI	23:41	TAU
10	TAU	3:03	GEM
12	GEM	8:17	CAN
14	CAN	16:27	LEO
17	LEO	3:37	VIR
19	VIR	16:19	LIB
22	LIB	3:57	SCO
24	SCO	12:48	SAG
26	SAG	18:29	CAP
28	CAP	21:51	AQU

JUL
1	AQU	0:08	PIS
3	PIS	2:23	ARI
5	ARI	5:23	TAU
7	TAU	9:42	GEM
9	GEM	15:54	CAN
12	CAN	0:28	LEO
14	LEO	11:28	VIR
17	VIR	0:04	LIB
19	LIB	12:17	SCO
22	SCO	21:59	SAG
24	SAG	4:07	CAP
26	CAP	7:03	AQU
28	AQU	8:07	PIS
30	PIS	8:56	ARI

AUG
1	ARI	10:57	TAU
3	TAU	15:10	GEM
5	GEM	21:59	CAN
8	CAN	7:16	LEO
10	LEO	18:33	VIR
13	VIR	7:08	LIB
15	LIB	19:43	SCO
18	SCO	6:30	SAG
20	SAG	13:53	CAP
22	CAP	17:29	AQU
24	AQU	18:12	PIS
26	PIS	17:46	ARI
28	ARI	18:10	TAU
30	TAU	21:07	GEM

SEP
2	GEM	3:30	CAN
4	CAN	13:05	LEO
7	LEO	0:47	VIR
9	VIR	13:27	LIB
12	LIB	2:05	SCO
14	SCO	13:32	SAG
16	SAG	22:21	CAP
19	CAP	3:30	AQU
21	AQU	5:06	PIS
23	PIS	4:31	ARI
25	ARI	3:45	TAU
27	TAU	5:01	GEM
29	GEM	9:56	CAN

OCT
1	CAN	18:53	LEO
4	LEO	6:40	VIR
6	VIR	19:28	LIB
9	LIB	7:56	SCO
11	SCO	19:19	SAG
14	SAG	4:51	CAP
16	CAP	11:34	AQU
18	AQU	14:55	PIS
20	PIS	15:27	ARI
22	ARI	14:47	TAU
24	TAU	15:04	GEM
26	GEM	18:24	CAN
29	CAN	1:55	LEO
31	LEO	13:04	VIR

NOV
3	VIR	1:51	LIB
5	LIB	14:12	SCO
8	SCO	1:06	SAG
10	SAG	10:18	CAP
12	CAP	17:31	AQU
14	AQU	22:35	PIS
17	PIS	0:35	ARI
19	ARI	1:15	TAU
21	TAU	1:54	GEM
23	GEM	4:31	CAN
25	CAN	10:40	LEO
27	LEO	20:41	VIR
30	VIR	9:06	LIB

DEC
2	LIB	21:30	SCO
5	SCO	8:09	SAG
7	SAG	16:33	CAP
9	CAP	22:59	AQU
12	AQU	3:46	PIS
14	PIS	7:06	ARI
16	ARI	9:22	TAU
18	TAU	11:27	GEM
20	GEM	14:40	CAN
22	CAN	20:23	LEO
25	LEO	5:24	VIR
27	VIR	17:11	LIB
30	LIB	5:43	SCO

— 102 —

LOVE SIGNS FOR BEGINNERS

—1954—

JAN
1	16:39	SAG
4	0:45	CAP
6	6:09	AQU
8	9:43	PIS
10	12:27	ARI
12	15:10	TAU
14	18:29	GEM
16	23:01	CAN
19	5:24	LEO
21	14:14	VIR
24	1:30	LIB
26	14:03	SCO
29	1:42	SAG
31	10:27	CAP

FEB
2	15:38	AQU
4	18:03	PIS
6	19:14	ARI
8	20:47	TAU
11	0:05	GEM
13	5:10	CAN
15	12:35	LEO
17	22:00	VIR
20	9:14	LIB
22	21:43	SCO
25	10:00	SAG
27	19:58	CAP

MAR
2	2:07	AQU
4	4:32	PIS
6	4:40	ARI
8	4:32	TAU
10	6:06	GEM
12	10:37	CAN
14	18:17	LEO
17	4:21	VIR
19	15:57	LIB
22	4:26	SCO
24	16:56	SAG
27	3:55	CAP
29	11:37	AQU
31	15:16	PIS

APR
2	15:40	ARI
4	14:43	TAU
6	14:40	GEM
8	17:29	CAN
11	0:05	LEO
13	10:03	VIR
15	21:58	LIB
18	10:32	SCO
20	22:55	SAG
23	10:11	CAP
25	19:02	AQU
28	0:21	PIS
30	2:08	ARI

MAY
2	1:42	TAU
4	1:06	GEM
6	2:30	CAN
8	7:29	LEO
10	16:23	VIR
13	4:03	LIB
15	16:42	SCO
18	4:53	SAG
20	15:49	CAP
23	0:48	AQU
25	7:08	PIS
27	10:32	ARI
29	11:33	TAU
31	11:40	GEM

JUN
2	12:46	CAN
4	16:34	LEO
7	0:06	VIR
9	11:37	LIB
12	0:15	SCO
14	12:05	SAG
16	22:35	CAP
19	6:26	AQU
21	12:37	PIS
23	16:44	ARI
25	19:09	TAU
27	20:41	GEM
29	22:35	CAN

JUL
2	2:16	LEO
4	8:56	VIR
6	19:04	LIB
9	19:19	SCO
11	19:40	SAG
14	13:19	CAP
16	22:07	AQU
19	0:52	PIS
21	3:30	ARI
23	6:41	TAU
25	11:10	GEM
27	17:49	CAN
29		LEO

AUG
3	3:14	LEO
5	15:03	VIR
8	3:32	LIB
10	14:20	SCO
13	21:54	SAG
15	2:17	CAP
17	4:37	AQU
19	6:26	PIS
21	8:56	ARI
23	12:50	TAU
25	18:22	GEM
28	1:44	CAN
30	11:12	LEO

SEP
1	22:49	SCO
4	11:32	SAG
6	23:10	CAP
9	7:31	AQU
11	11:55	PIS
13	13:22	ARI
15	13:44	TAU
17	14:55	GEM
19	18:13	CAN
22	0:48	LEO
24	11:11	VIR
26	18:11	LIB
29	5:52	SCO

OCT
1	18:41	SAG
4	7:04	CAP
6	16:45	AQU
8	22:17	PIS
10	23:58	ARI
12	23:32	TAU
14	23:10	GEM
17	0:50	CAN
19	5:41	LEO
21	13:44	VIR
24	0:12	LIB
26	12:11	SCO
29	0:59	SAG
31	13:36	CAP

NOV
3	0:22	AQU
5	7:34	PIS
7	10:42	ARI
9	10:48	TAU
11	9:50	GEM
13	9:59	CAN
15	13:02	LEO
17	19:52	VIR
20	6:02	LIB
22	18:13	SCO
25	7:01	SAG
27	19:24	CAP
30	6:19	AQU

DEC
2	14:38	PIS
4	19:35	ARI
6	21:23	TAU
8	21:16	GEM
10	21:06	CAN
12	22:48	LEO
15	3:54	VIR
17	12:51	LIB
20	0:43	SCO
22	13:35	SAG
25	1:40	CAP
27	12:00	AQU
29	20:09	PIS

—1955—

JAN
1	1:56	ARI
3	5:24	TAU
5	7:04	GEM
7	8:00	CAN
9	9:41	LEO
11	13:43	VIR
13	21:15	LIB
16	8:15	SCO
18	21:01	SAG
21	9:09	CAP
23	18:58	AQU
26	2:11	PIS
28	7:19	ARI
30	11:06	TAU

FEB
1	14:02	GEM
3	16:36	CAN
5	19:28	LEO
7	23:43	VIR
10	6:33	LIB
12	16:38	SCO
15	5:07	SAG
17	17:34	CAP
20	3:33	AQU
22	10:09	PIS
24	14:06	ARI
26	16:46	TAU
28	19:24	GEM

MAR
2	22:40	CAN
5	2:48	LEO
7	8:09	VIR
9	15:20	LIB
12	1:04	SCO
14	13:13	SAG
17	2:01	CAP
19	12:47	AQU
21	19:45	PIS
23	23:09	ARI
26	0:31	TAU
28	1:42	GEM
30	4:05	CAN

APR
1	8:20	LEO
3	14:31	VIR
5	22:34	LIB
8	8:38	SCO
10	20:41	SAG
13	9:40	CAP
15	21:20	AQU
18	5:28	PIS
20	9:29	ARI
22	10:24	TAU
24	10:29	GEM
26	11:09	CAN
28	14:08	LEO
30	19:58	VIR

MAY
3	4:26	LIB
5	15:04	SCO
8	3:19	SAG
10	16:19	CAP
13	4:29	AQU
15	13:53	PIS
17	19:21	ARI
19	21:12	TAU
21	20:56	GEM
23	20:33	CAN
25	21:52	LEO
28	2:16	VIR
30	10:08	LIB

JUN
1	20:54	SCO
4	9:24	SAG
6	22:21	CAP
9	10:30	AQU
11	20:32	PIS
14	3:24	ARI
16	6:50	TAU
18	7:37	GEM
20	7:15	CAN
22	7:36	LEO
24	10:26	VIR
26	16:55	LIB
29	3:04	SCO

JUL
1	15:34	SAG
4	4:29	CAP
6	16:18	AQU
9	2:09	PIS
11	9:33	ARI
13	14:20	TAU
15	16:43	GEM
17	17:30	CAN
19	18:03	LEO
21	20:06	VIR
24	1:16	LIB
26	10:19	SCO
28	22:24	SAG
31	11:19	CAP

AUG
2	22:52	AQU
5	8:04	PIS
7	15:00	ARI
9	20:03	TAU
11	23:33	GEM
14	1:50	CAN
16	3:34	LEO
18	5:57	VIR
20	10:37	LIB
22	18:37	SCO
25	6:03	SAG
27	18:57	CAP
30	6:35	AQU

SEP
1	15:23	PIS
3	21:24	ARI
6	1:36	TAU
8	4:58	GEM
10	8:01	CAN
12	11:02	LEO
14	14:33	VIR
16	19:35	LIB
19	3:18	SCO
21	14:11	SAG
24	3:01	CAP
26	15:07	AQU
29	0:12	PIS

OCT
1	5:46	ARI
3	8:52	TAU
5	10:59	GEM
7	13:23	CAN
9	16:41	LEO
11	21:11	VIR
14	3:13	LIB
16	11:23	SCO
18	22:07	SAG
21	10:52	CAP
23	23:33	AQU
26	9:37	PIS
28	15:46	ARI
30	18:30	TAU

NOV
1	19:23	GEM
3	20:11	CAN
5	22:20	LEO
8	2:36	VIR
10	9:15	LIB
12	18:12	SCO
15	17:59	SAG
17	18:10	CAP
20	6:58	AQU
22	18:10	PIS
25	1:47	ARI
27	5:27	TAU
29	6:11	GEM

DEC
1	5:46	CAN
3	6:07	LEO
5	8:50	VIR
7	14:48	LIB
9	23:59	SCO
12	11:34	SAG
15	0:23	CAP
17	13:19	AQU
20	1:02	PIS
22	10:05	ARI
24	15:33	TAU
26	17:33	GEM
28	17:17	CAN
30	16:36	LEO

LOVE SIGNS FOR BEGINNERS

—1957—

JAN
2	17:25	AQU
5	6:04	PIS
7	18:23	ARI
10	4:27	TAU
12	13:06	GEM
14	18:03	CAN
16	12:50	LEO
18	12:03	VIR
20	12:55	LIB
22	0:52	SCO
25	11:32	SAG
27	11:32	CAP
29	23:42	AQU

FEB
1	12:20	PIS
4	0:42	ARI
6	11:37	TAU
8	19:34	GEM
10	23:39	CAN
13	0:19	LEO
15	23:17	VIR
16	22:50	LIB
20	1:06	SCO
22	7:23	SAG
24	17:27	CAP
26	5:42	AQU
28	18:25	PIS

MAR
3	6:31	ARI
5	17:20	TAU
8	2:03	GEM
10	7:45	CAN
12	10:12	LEO
14	10:20	VIR
16	9:59	LIB
18	11:15	SCO
20	15:53	SAG
23	0:34	CAP
25	12:17	AQU
28	1:00	PIS
30	12:55	ARI

APR
1	23:11	TAU
4	7:30	GEM
6	13:37	CAN
8	17:24	LEO
10	19:13	VIR
12	20:08	LIB
14	21:45	SCO
17	1:43	SAG
19	9:08	CAP
21	19:53	AQU
24	8:23	PIS
26	20:22	ARI
29	6:18	TAU

MAY
1	13:47	GEM
3	19:08	CAN
5	22:54	LEO
8	1:37	VIR
10	3:57	LIB
12	6:48	SCO
14	11:13	SAG
16	18:13	CAP
19	4:12	AQU
21	16:20	PIS
24	4:34	ARI
26	14:43	TAU
28	21:47	GEM
31	2:05	CAN

JUN
2	4:45	LEO
4	6:59	VIR
6	9:45	LIB
8	13:41	SCO
10	19:09	SAG
13	2:36	CAP
15	12:23	AQU
18	0:15	PIS
20	12:46	ARI
22	23:38	TAU
25	7:07	GEM
27	11:01	CAN
29	12:31	LEO

JUL
1	13:23	VIR
3	15:16	LIB
5	19:10	SCO
8	1:20	SAG
10	9:35	CAP
12	19:43	AQU
15	7:32	PIS
17	20:14	ARI
20	7:58	TAU
22	16:34	GEM
24	21:05	CAN
26	22:16	LEO
28	21:59	VIR
30	22:20	LIB

AUG
2	1:01	SCO
4	6:47	SAG
6	15:23	CAP
9	2:01	AQU
11	14:02	PIS
14	2:46	ARI
16	15:00	TAU
19	0:51	GEM
21	6:48	CAN
23	8:51	LEO
25	8:26	VIR
27	7:41	LIB
29	8:45	SCO
31	13:07	SAG

SEP
2	21:05	CAP
5	7:50	AQU
7	20:04	PIS
10	8:45	ARI
12	20:57	TAU
15	7:26	GEM
17	14:50	CAN
19	18:31	LEO
21	19:11	VIR
23	18:33	LIB
25	18:40	SCO
27	21:27	SAG
30	3:59	CAP

OCT
2	14:04	AQU
5	2:17	PIS
7	14:57	ARI
10	2:48	TAU
12	13:01	GEM
14	20:54	CAN
17	1:59	LEO
19	4:24	VIR
21	5:03	LIB
23	5:31	SCO
25	7:33	SAG
27	12:41	CAP
29	21:32	AQU

NOV
1	9:18	PIS
3	22:00	ARI
6	9:38	TAU
8	19:09	GEM
11	2:24	CAN
13	7:36	LEO
15	11:07	VIR
17	13:25	LIB
19	15:17	SCO
21	17:52	SAG
23	22:29	CAP
26	6:16	AQU
28	17:16	PIS

DEC
1	5:56	ARI
3	17:48	TAU
6	3:00	GEM
8	9:16	CAN
10	13:23	LEO
12	16:28	VIR
14	19:23	LIB
16	22:35	SCO
19	2:30	SAG
21	7:47	CAP
23	15:19	AQU
26	1:41	PIS
28	14:13	ARI
31	2:37	TAU

—1956—

JAN
1	17:31	VIR
3	21:44	LIB
6	6:00	SCO
8	17:32	SAG
11	6:33	CAP
13	19:19	AQU
16	6:47	PIS
18	16:17	ARI
20	23:11	TAU
23	3:06	GEM
25	4:20	CAN
27	4:06	LEO
29	4:17	VIR
31	6:56	LIB

FEB
2	13:33	SCO
5	0:13	SAG
7	13:08	CAP
10	1:52	AQU
12	12:52	PIS
14	21:48	ARI
17	4:48	TAU
19	9:50	GEM
21	12:50	CAN
23	14:10	LEO
25	15:05	VIR
27	17:20	LIB
29	22:45	SCO

MAR
3	8:09	SAG
5	20:32	CAP
8	9:19	AQU
10	20:11	PIS
13	4:26	ARI
15	10:32	TAU
17	15:11	GEM
19	18:47	CAN
21	21:31	LEO
23	23:53	VIR
26	3:00	LIB
28	8:18	SCO
30	16:56	SAG

APR
2	4:37	CAP
4	17:24	AQU
7	4:37	PIS
9	12:47	ARI
11	21:30	TAU
13	18:03	GEM
16	0:15	CAN
18	3:00	LEO
20	6:17	VIR
22	10:36	LIB
24	16:44	SCO
27	1:25	SAG
29	12:44	CAP

MAY
2	1:27	AQU
4	13:15	PIS
6	22:06	ARI
9	3:24	TAU
11	6:00	GEM
13	7:21	CAN
15	8:52	LEO
17	11:40	VIR
19	16:17	LIB
21	23:26	SCO
24	8:46	SAG
26	20:11	CAP
29	8:52	AQU
31	21:09	PIS

JUN
3	7:05	ARI
5	13:22	TAU
7	16:09	GEM
9	16:42	CAN
11	16:45	LEO
13	18:03	VIR
15	21:58	LIB
18	5:03	SCO
20	14:55	SAG
23	2:43	CAP
25	15:26	AQU
28	3:54	PIS
30	14:43	ARI

JUL
2	22:26	TAU
5	2:26	GEM
7	3:20	CAN
9	2:42	LEO
11	2:34	VIR
13	4:54	LIB
15	10:56	SCO
17	20:38	SAG
20	8:41	CAP
22	21:28	AQU
25	9:50	PIS
27	20:54	ARI
30	5:40	TAU

AUG
1	11:16	GEM
3	13:32	CAN
5	12:50	LEO
7	12:50	VIR
9	13:50	LIB
11	18:20	SCO
14	2:47	SAG
16	14:47	CAP
19	3:38	AQU
21	15:47	PIS
24	2:30	ARI
26	11:23	TAU
28	17:59	GEM
30	21:51	CAN

SEP
1	23:14	LEO
3	23:20	VIR
6	0:04	LIB
8	3:26	SCO
10	10:46	SAG
12	21:46	CAP
15	10:28	AQU
17	22:34	PIS
20	8:47	ARI
22	17:01	TAU
24	23:25	GEM
27	4:00	CAN
29	6:49	LEO

OCT
1	8:24	VIR
3	10:01	LIB
5	13:19	SCO
7	19:46	SAG
10	5:48	CAP
12	18:09	AQU
15	6:35	PIS
17	6:25	ARI
20	0:07	TAU
22	5:29	GEM
24	9:23	CAN
26	12:27	LEO
28	15:09	VIR
30	18:10	LIB

NOV
1	22:24	SCO
4	4:56	SAG
6	14:24	CAP
9	2:19	AQU
11	14:51	PIS
14	1:36	ARI
16	9:12	TAU
18	13:45	GEM
20	16:18	CAN
22	18:10	LEO
24	20:32	VIR
27	0:11	LIB
29	5:34	SCO

DEC
1	12:59	SAG
3	22:36	CAP
6	10:16	AQU
8	22:57	PIS
11	10:37	ARI
13	19:16	TAU
16	0:06	GEM
18	1:52	CAN
20	2:11	LEO
22	2:56	VIR
24	5:39	LIB
26	11:09	SCO
28	19:20	SAG
31	5:37	CAP

— 104 —

—1958—

JAN
2	12:21	GEM
4	18:22	LEO
6	21:21	LEO
8	22:59	VIR
11	0:52	LIB
13	4:02	SCO
15	8:49	SAG
17	15:13	CAP
19	23:22	AQU
22	9:41	PIS
24	22:03	ARI
27	10:56	TAU
29	21:47	GEM

FEB
3	4:41	CAN
5	7:38	LEO
7	8:11	VIR
9	8:23	LIB
11	10:03	SCO
13	14:11	SAG
15	20:55	CAP
18	5:51	AQU
20	16:39	PIS
23	5:02	ARI
25	18:05	TAU
28	5:52	GEM

MAR
2	14:17	CAN
4	18:27	LEO
6	19:15	VIR
8	18:35	LIB
10	18:34	SCO
12	20:56	SAG
15	2:36	CAP
17	11:28	AQU
19	22:41	PIS
22	11:17	ARI
25	0:16	TAU
27	12:20	GEM
30	21:53	CAN
	3:46	LEO

APR
1	6:01	VIR
3	6:05	LIB
5	5:16	SCO
7	6:07	SAG
9	10:00	CAP
11	17:41	AQU
14	4:38	PIS
16	17:23	ARI
19	6:16	TAU
21	18:03	GEM
24	3:46	CAN
26	10:44	LEO
28	14:41	VIR
30	16:06	LIB

MAY
2	16:14	SCO
4	16:43	SAG
6	19:21	CAP
9	1:19	AQU
11	11:27	PIS
13	23:56	ARI
16	12:50	TAU
19	0:14	GEM
21	9:23	CAN
23	16:15	LEO
25	21:00	VIR
27	23:55	LIB
30	1:33	SCO

JUN
3	2:54	SAG
5	5:23	CAP
7	10:34	AQU
9	19:24	PIS
12	7:20	ARI
14	20:12	TAU
17	7:31	GEM
19	16:04	CAN
21	22:04	LEO
24	2:22	VIR
26	5:42	LIB
28	8:30	SCO
30	11:12	SAG
	14:32	CAP

JUL
2	19:44	SAG
5	3:57	CAP
7	15:18	AQU
10	4:09	PIS
12	15:47	ARI
15	5:31	TAU
17	8:42	GEM
19	11:11	CAN
21	13:57	LEO
23	17:25	VIR
26	21:53	LIB
28	3:52	SCO
30		SAG

AUG
1	12:11	PIS
3	23:14	ARI
6	12:04	TAU
9	0:16	GEM
11	9:25	CAN
13	14:43	LEO
15	17:07	VIR
17	19:50	LIB
19	22:48	SCO
22	3:38	SAG
24	10:28	CAP
26	19:25	AQU
29	6:35	PIS

SEP
2	19:24	TAU
5	8:07	GEM
7	18:22	CAN
10	0:42	LEO
12	3:19	VIR
14	3:44	LIB
16	3:49	SCO
18	5:16	SAG
20	9:13	CAP
22	16:03	AQU
25	1:33	PIS
27	13:07	ARI
30	1:58	TAU

OCT
2	14:50	GEM
5	2:00	CAN
7	9:51	LEO
9	13:49	VIR
11	14:44	LIB
13	14:11	SCO
15	14:09	SAG
17	16:23	CAP
19	22:04	AQU
22	7:19	PIS
24	19:10	ARI
27	8:07	TAU
29	20:49	GEM

NOV
1	8:09	CAN
3	17:02	LEO
5	22:45	VIR
8	1:16	LIB
10	1:30	SCO
12	1:03	SAG
14	1:54	CAP
16	5:53	AQU
18	13:56	PIS
21	1:28	ARI
23	14:30	TAU
26	3:51	GEM
28	13:51	CAN
30	22:41	LEO

DEC
3	5:18	VIR
5	9:31	LIB
7	11:28	SCO
9	12:02	SAG
11	12:46	CAP
13	15:38	AQU
15	22:12	PIS
18	8:45	ARI
20	21:38	TAU
23	10:09	GEM
25	20:33	CAN
28	4:33	LEO
30	10:41	VIR

—1959—

JAN
1	15:21	LIB
3	18:42	SCO
5	20:56	SAG
7	22:50	CAP
10	1:51	AQU
12	7:39	PIS
14	17:09	ARI
17	5:33	TAU
19	18:16	GEM
22	4:47	CAN
24	12:13	LEO
26	17:13	VIR
28	20:54	LIB
31	0:05	SCO

FEB
2	3:11	SAG
4	6:29	CAP
6	10:40	AQU
8	16:50	PIS
11	1:55	ARI
13	13:47	TAU
16	2:39	GEM
18	13:51	CAN
20	21:38	LEO
23	2:06	VIR
25	4:29	LIB
27	6:14	SCO

MAR
1	8:33	SAG
3	12:06	CAP
5	17:16	AQU
8	0:25	PIS
10	9:53	ARI
12	21:37	TAU
15	10:31	GEM
17	22:28	CAN
20	7:22	LEO
22	12:28	VIR
24	14:27	LIB
26	14:53	SCO
28	15:31	SAG
30	17:49	CAP

APR
1	22:41	AQU
4	6:23	PIS
6	16:33	ARI
9	4:32	TAU
11	17:25	GEM
14	5:48	CAN
16	15:55	LEO
18	22:28	VIR
21	1:19	LIB
23	1:34	SCO
25	0:59	SAG
27	1:32	CAP
29	4:55	AQU

MAY
1	11:58	PIS
3	22:19	ARI
6	10:39	TAU
8	23:34	GEM
11	11:57	CAN
13	22:40	LEO
16	6:38	VIR
18	11:06	LIB
20	12:24	SCO
22	11:51	SAG
24	11:24	CAP
26	13:09	AQU
28	18:42	PIS
31	4:18	ARI

JUN
2	16:37	TAU
5	5:35	GEM
7	17:44	CAN
10	4:19	LEO
12	12:50	VIR
14	18:42	LIB
16	21:38	SCO
18	22:14	SAG
20	22:01	CAP
23	23:00	AQU
25	3:09	PIS
27	11:28	ARI
29	23:11	TAU

JUL
2	12:05	GEM
5	0:03	CAN
7	10:08	LEO
9	18:15	VIR
12	0:26	LIB
14	4:33	SCO
16	6:42	SAG
18	7:42	CAP
20	9:05	AQU
22	12:41	PIS
24	19:53	ARI
27	6:43	TAU
29	19:23	GEM

AUG
1	7:24	CAN
3	17:09	LEO
6	0:29	VIR
8	5:56	LIB
10	10:00	SCO
12	12:58	SAG
14	15:18	CAP
16	17:53	AQU
18	21:59	PIS
21	4:51	ARI
23	14:58	TAU
26	3:18	GEM
28	15:33	CAN
31	1:33	LEO

SEP
2	8:31	VIR
4	12:56	LIB
6	15:53	SCO
8	18:20	SAG
10	21:04	CAP
13	0:43	AQU
15	5:54	PIS
17	13:12	ARI
19	23:12	TAU
22	11:16	GEM
24	23:49	CAN
27	10:36	LEO
29	18:04	VIR

OCT
1	22:08	LIB
3	23:54	SCO
6	0:54	SAG
8	2:38	CAP
10	6:12	AQU
12	12:06	PIS
14	20:20	ARI
17	6:40	TAU
19	18:40	GEM
22	7:22	CAN
24	19:03	LEO
27	3:48	VIR
29	8:41	LIB
31	10:14	SCO

NOV
2	10:02	SAG
4	10:05	CAP
6	12:14	AQU
8	17:35	PIS
11	1:30	ARI
13	13:04	TAU
16	1:16	GEM
18	13:56	CAN
21	2:04	LEO
23	12:08	VIR
25	18:41	LIB
27	21:22	SCO
29	21:12	SAG

DEC
1	20:11	CAP
3	20:35	AQU
6	0:16	PIS
8	7:59	ARI
10	18:56	TAU
13	7:24	GEM
15	20:00	CAN
18	7:58	LEO
20	18:29	VIR
23	2:29	LIB
25	7:01	SCO
27	8:16	SAG
29	7:38	CAP
31	7:15	AQU

LOVE SIGNS FOR BEGINNERS

—1960—

JAN
2	9:19	PIS	
5	15:21	ARI	
7	1:22	TAU	
9	13:45	GEM	
12	2:23	CAN	
14	13:59	LEO	
17	0:03	VIR	
19	8:14	LIB	
21	13:59	SCO	
23	17:03	SAG	
25	18:00	CAP	
27	18:19	AQU	
29	19:56	PIS	

FEB
1	0:39	ARI	
3	9:16	TAU	
5	20:58	GEM	
8	9:37	CAN	
10	21:08	LEO	
13	6:35	VIR	
15	13:55	LIB	
17	19:24	SCO	
19	23:12	SAG	
22	1:39	CAP	
24	3:00	AQU	
26	6:04	PIS	
28	10:37	ARI	

MAR
1	18:18	TAU	
4	5:08	GEM	
6	17:37	CAN	
9	5:25	LEO	
11	14:47	VIR	
13	21:19	LIB	
16	1:37	SCO	
18	4:37	SAG	
20	7:14	CAP	
22	10:10	AQU	
24	14:02	PIS	
26	19:29	ARI	
29	3:13	TAU	
31	13:32	GEM	

APR
3	1:46	CAN	
5	14:01	LEO	
8	0:02	VIR	
10	6:36	LIB	
12	10:01	SCO	
14	11:37	SAG	
16	13:01	CAP	
18	15:32	AQU	
20	19:55	PIS	
23	2:23	ARI	
25	10:50	TAU	
27	21:16	GEM	
30	9:22	CAN	

MAY
2	21:59	LEO	
5	8:59	VIR	
7	16:30	LIB	
9	20:07	SCO	
11	20:55	SAG	
13	20:50	CAP	
15	21:51	AQU	
18	1:23	PIS	
20	7:55	ARI	
22	17:00	TAU	
25	3:55	GEM	
27	16:06	CAN	
30	4:50	LEO	

JUN
1	16:38	VIR	
4	1:31	LIB	
6	6:20	SCO	
8	7:31	SAG	
10	6:48	CAP	
12	6:23	AQU	
14	8:17	PIS	
16	13:42	ARI	
18	22:33	TAU	
21	9:46	GEM	
23	22:10	CAN	
26	10:51	LEO	
28	22:53	VIR	

JUL
1	8:46	LIB	
3	15:08	SCO	
5	17:42	SAG	
7	17:34	CAP	
9	16:43	AQU	
11	17:19	PIS	
13	21:07	ARI	
16	4:48	TAU	
18	15:40	GEM	
21	4:09	CAN	
23	16:46	LEO	
26	4:31	VIR	
28	14:33	LIB	
30	21:55	SCO	

AUG
2	2:04	SAG	
4	3:26	CAP	
6	3:21	AQU	
8	3:42	PIS	
10	6:21	ARI	
12	12:36	TAU	
14	22:29	GEM	
17	10:43	CAN	
19	23:18	LEO	
22	10:41	VIR	
24	20:09	LIB	
27	3:24	SCO	
29	8:19	SAG	
31	11:09	CAP	

SEP
2	12:35	AQU	
4	13:51	PIS	
6	16:26	ARI	
8	21:44	TAU	
11	6:31	GEM	
13	18:10	CAN	
16	6:46	LEO	
18	18:07	VIR	
21	2:58	LIB	
23	9:18	SCO	
25	13:42	SAG	
27	16:54	CAP	
29	19:32	AQU	

OCT
1	22:14	PIS	
4	1:46	ARI	
6	7:09	TAU	
8	15:16	GEM	
11	2:18	CAN	
13	14:55	LEO	
16	2:40	VIR	
18	11:32	LIB	
20	17:06	SCO	
22	20:16	SAG	
24	22:28	CAP	
27	0:57	AQU	
29	4:26	PIS	
31	9:11	ARI	

NOV
2	15:27	TAU	
4	23:44	GEM	
7	10:26	CAN	
9	22:59	LEO	
12	11:24	VIR	
14	21:07	LIB	
17	2:53	SCO	
19	5:17	SAG	
21	6:02	CAP	
23	7:04	AQU	
25	9:49	PIS	
27	14:51	ARI	
29	22:00	TAU	

DEC
2	7:01	GEM	
4	17:52	CAN	
7	6:21	LEO	
9	19:13	VIR	
12	6:10	LIB	
14	13:13	SCO	
16	16:07	SAG	
18	16:16	CAP	
20	15:49	AQU	
22	16:47	PIS	
24	20:34	ARI	
27	3:30	TAU	
29	13:01	GEM	

—1961—

JAN
1	0:22	CAN	
3	12:54	LEO	
6	1:48	VIR	
8	13:31	LIB	
10	22:09	SCO	
13	2:40	SAG	
15	3:41	CAP	
17	2:55	AQU	
19	2:32	PIS	
21	4:26	ARI	
23	9:51	TAU	
25	18:50	GEM	
28	6:22	CAN	
30	19:05	LEO	

FEB
2	7:48	VIR	
4	19:27	LIB	
7	4:51	SCO	
9	11:01	SAG	
11	13:51	CAP	
13	14:14	AQU	
15	13:53	PIS	
17	14:41	ARI	
19	18:21	TAU	
22	1:51	GEM	
24	12:49	CAN	
27	1:34	LEO	

MAR
1	14:12	VIR	
4	1:21	LIB	
6	10:24	SCO	
8	17:04	SAG	
10	21:13	CAP	
12	23:29	AQU	
15	0:26	PIS	
17	1:32	ARI	
19	4:25	TAU	
21	10:32	GEM	
23	20:22	CAN	
26	8:48	LEO	
28	21:30	VIR	
31	8:21	LIB	

APR
2	16:36	SCO	
4	22:34	SAG	
7	2:52	CAP	
9	6:03	AQU	
11	8:31	PIS	
13	10:55	ARI	
15	14:16	TAU	
17	19:55	GEM	
20	4:50	CAN	
22	16:43	LEO	
25	5:31	VIR	
27	16:34	LIB	
30	0:27	SCO	

MAY
2	5:25	SAG	
4	8:40	CAP	
6	11:24	AQU	
8	14:23	PIS	
10	17:56	ARI	
12	22:25	TAU	
15	4:34	GEM	
17	13:17	CAN	
20	0:45	LEO	
22	13:38	VIR	
25	1:18	LIB	
27	9:34	SCO	
29	14:11	SAG	
31	16:20	CAP	

JUN
2	17:45	AQU	
4	19:50	PIS	
6	23:23	ARI	
9	4:38	TAU	
11	11:40	GEM	
13	20:50	CAN	
16	8:16	LEO	
18	21:12	VIR	
21	9:32	LIB	
23	18:51	SCO	
26	0:05	SAG	
28	2:00	CAP	
30	2:18	AQU	

JUL
2	2:52	PIS	
4	5:12	ARI	
6	10:01	TAU	
8	17:27	GEM	
11	3:13	CAN	
13	14:56	LEO	
16	3:55	VIR	
18	16:39	LIB	
21	3:05	SCO	
23	9:42	SAG	
25	12:29	CAP	
27	12:41	AQU	
29	12:56	PIS	

AUG
2	16:19	TAU	
4	23:04	GEM	
7	8:56	CAN	
9	20:59	LEO	
12	10:00	VIR	
14	22:44	LIB	
17	9:44	SCO	
19	17:44	SAG	
22	22:07	CAP	
24	23:25	AQU	
27	23:02	PIS	
29	22:49	ARI	
31	0:37	TAU	

SEP
3	5:52	GEM	
5	15:00	CAN	
8	3:01	LEO	
10	16:05	VIR	
13	4:33	LIB	
15	15:23	SCO	
17	23:54	SAG	
20	5:42	CAP	
22	8:43	AQU	
24	9:36	PIS	
26	9:40	ARI	
28	10:42	TAU	
30	14:31	GEM	

OCT
3	9:43	LEO	
5	22:45	VIR	
8	11:04	LIB	
10	21:19	SCO	
13	5:21	SAG	
15	11:24	CAP	
17	15:37	AQU	
19	18:10	PIS	
21	19:36	ARI	
23	21:07	TAU	
26	0:24	GEM	
28	7:03	CAN	
30	17:30	LEO	

NOV
2	6:17	VIR	
4	18:42	LIB	
7	4:40	SCO	
9	11:51	SAG	
11	16:59	CAP	
13	20:59	AQU	
16	0:18	PIS	
18	3:10	ARI	
20	6:03	TAU	
22	9:59	GEM	
24	16:20	CAN	
27	2:01	LEO	
29	14:25	VIR	

DEC
2	3:08	LIB	
4	13:30	SCO	
6	20:25	SAG	
9	0:31	CAP	
11	3:11	AQU	
13	5:41	PIS	
15	8:44	ARI	
17	12:39	TAU	
19	17:47	GEM	
22	0:50	CAN	
24	10:26	LEO	
26	22:29	VIR	
29	11:26	LIB	
31	22:42	SCO	

LOVE SIGNS FOR BEGINNERS

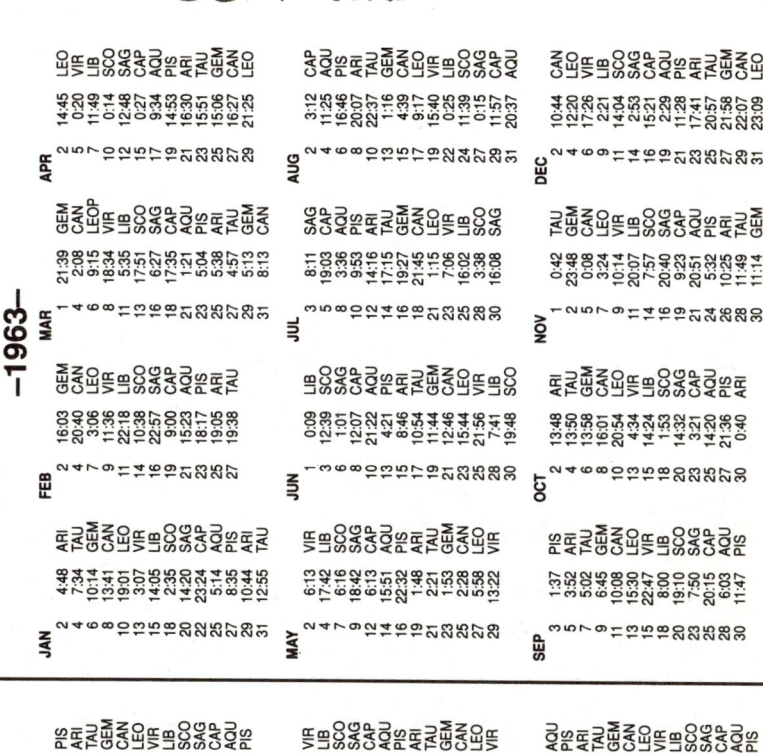

—1962—

JAN
3	6:23	SAG
5	10:24	CAP
7	12:00	AQU
9	12:53	PIS
11	14:34	ARI
13	18:01	TAU
15	23:42	GEM
18	7:39	CAN
20	17:50	LEO
23	5:53	VIR
25	18:52	LIB
28	6:54	SCO
30	15:59	SAG

FEB
1	21:10	CAP
3	22:57	AQU
5	22:53	PIS
7	22:50	ARI
10	0:35	TAU
12	5:18	GEM
14	13:20	CAN
17	0:04	LEO
19	12:27	VIR
22	1:22	LIB
24	13:36	SCO
26	23:46	SAG

MAR
1	6:38	CAP
3	9:52	AQU
5	10:16	PIS
7	9:40	ARI
9	9:32	TAU
11	12:35	GEM
13	19:25	CAN
16	5:56	LEO
18	18:33	VIR
21	7:28	LIB
23	19:29	SCO
26	5:49	SAG
28	13:58	CAP
30	18:43	AQU

APR
1	20:42	PIS
3	20:41	ARI
5	20:25	TAU
7	22:00	GEM
10	3:12	CAN
12	12:36	LEO
15	0:57	VIR
17	13:54	LIB
20	1:37	SCO
22	11:27	SAG
24	19:20	CAP
27	1:08	AQU
29	4:40	PIS

MAY
1	6:12	ARI
3	6:49	TAU
5	8:16	GEM
7	12:28	CAN
9	20:35	LEO
12	8:11	VIR
14	21:03	LIB
17	8:43	SCO
19	18:02	SAG
22	1:08	CAP
24	6:31	AQU
26	10:29	PIS
28	13:15	ARI
30	15:17	TAU

JUN
1	17:40	GEM
3	21:56	CAN
6	5:23	LEO
8	16:12	VIR
11	4:51	LIB
13	16:45	SCO
16	2:03	SAG
18	8:30	CAP
20	12:49	AQU
22	15:59	PIS
24	18:43	ARI
26	21:34	TAU
29	1:09	GEM

JUL
1	6:19	CAN
3	13:55	LEO
6	0:22	VIR
8	12:48	LIB
11	1:05	SCO
13	11:00	SAG
15	17:32	CAP
17	21:07	AQU
19	23:00	PIS
22	0:34	ARI
24	2:57	TAU
26	6:57	GEM
28	13:00	CAN
30	21:21	LEO

AUG
2	7:57	VIR
4	20:17	LIB
7	8:56	SCO
9	19:48	SAG
12	3:18	CAP
14	7:07	AQU
16	8:17	PIS
18	8:25	ARI
20	9:20	TAU
22	12:28	GEM
24	18:34	CAN
27	3:30	LEO
29	14:36	VIR

SEP
1	3:01	LIB
3	15:46	SCO
6	3:26	SAG
8	12:20	CAP
10	17:26	AQU
12	19:02	PIS
14	18:33	ARI
16	18:00	TAU
18	19:29	GEM
21	0:26	CAN
23	9:07	LEO
25	20:31	VIR
28	3:49	LIB
30	21:49	SCO

OCT
3	9:40	SAG
5	19:35	CAP
8	2:22	AQU
10	5:29	PIS
12	5:41	ARI
14	4:43	TAU
16	4:50	GEM
18	8:05	CAN
20	15:30	LEO
23	2:31	VIR
25	15:14	LIB
28	3:49	SCO
30	15:19	SAG

NOV
2	1:17	CAP
4	9:02	AQU
6	13:52	PIS
8	15:45	ARI
10	15:45	TAU
12	15:43	GEM
14	17:49	CAN
16	23:40	LEO
19	9:33	VIR
21	21:58	LIB
24	10:33	SCO
26	21:43	SAG
29	7:00	CAP

DEC
1	14:26	AQU
3	19:53	PIS
5	23:17	ARI
8	0:59	TAU
10	2:07	GEM
12	4:21	CAN
14	9:20	LEO
16	17:59	VIR
19	5:41	LIB
21	18:18	SCO
24	5:33	SAG
26	14:19	CAP
28	20:42	AQU
31	1:20	PIS

—1963—

JAN
2	4:48	ARI
4	7:34	TAU
6	10:14	GEM
8	13:41	CAN
10	19:01	LEO
13	3:07	VIR
15	14:05	LIB
18	2:35	SCO
20	14:20	SAG
22	23:24	CAP
25	5:14	AQU
27	8:35	PIS
29	10:44	ARI
31	12:55	TAU

FEB
2	16:03	GEM
4	20:40	CAN
7	3:06	LEO
9	11:36	VIR
11	22:18	LIB
14	10:38	SCO
16	22:57	SAG
19	9:00	CAP
21	15:23	AQU
23	18:17	PIS
25	19:05	ARI
27	19:38	TAU

MAR
1	21:39	GEM
4	2:08	CAN
6	9:15	LEOP
8	18:34	VIR
11	5:35	LIB
13	17:51	SCO
16	6:27	SAG
18	17:35	CAP
21	1:21	AQU
23	5:04	PIS
25	5:38	ARI
27	4:57	TAU
29	5:13	GEM
31	8:13	CAN

APR
2	14:45	LEO
5	0:20	VIR
7	11:49	LIB
10	0:14	SCO
12	12:48	SAG
15	0:27	CAP
17	9:34	AQU
19	14:53	PIS
21	16:30	ARI
23	15:51	TAU
25	15:06	GEM
27	16:27	CAN
29	21:25	LEO

MAY
2	6:13	VIR
4	17:42	LIB
7	6:16	SCO
9	18:42	SAG
12	6:13	CAP
14	15:51	AQU
16	22:32	PIS
19	1:48	ARI
21	2:21	TAU
23	1:53	GEM
25	2:28	CAN
27	5:58	LEO
29	13:22	VIR

JUN
1	0:09	LIB
3	12:39	SCO
6	1:01	SAG
8	12:07	CAP
10	21:22	AQU
13	4:21	PIS
15	8:46	ARI
17	10:54	TAU
19	11:44	GEM
21	12:46	CAN
23	15:44	LEO
25	21:56	VIR
28	7:41	LIB
30	19:48	SCO

JUL
3	8:11	SAG
5	19:03	CAP
8	3:36	AQU
10	9:53	PIS
12	14:16	ARI
14	17:15	TAU
16	19:27	GEM
18	21:45	CAN
21	1:15	LEO
23	7:06	VIR
25	16:02	LIB
28	3:38	SCO
30	16:08	SAG

AUG
2	3:12	CAP
4	11:25	AQU
6	16:46	PIS
8	20:07	ARI
10	22:37	TAU
13	1:16	GEM
15	4:39	CAN
17	9:17	LEO
19	15:40	VIR
22	0:25	LIB
24	11:39	SCO
27	0:15	SAG
29	11:57	CAP
31	20:37	AQU

SEP
3	1:37	PIS
5	3:52	ARI
7	5:02	TAU
9	6:45	GEM
11	10:08	CAN
13	15:30	LEO
15	22:47	VIR
18	8:00	LIB
20	19:10	SCO
23	7:50	SAG
25	20:15	CAP
28	6:03	AQU
30	11:47	PIS

OCT
2	13:48	ARI
4	13:50	TAU
6	13:58	GEM
8	16:01	CAN
10	20:54	LEO
13	4:34	VIR
15	14:24	LIB
18	1:53	SCO
20	14:32	SAG
23	3:21	CAP
25	14:20	AQU
27	21:36	PIS
30	0:40	ARI

NOV
1	0:42	TAU
2	23:48	GEM
5	0:08	CAN
7	3:24	LEO
9	10:14	VIR
11	20:07	LIB
14	7:57	SCO
16	20:40	SAG
19	9:23	CAP
21	20:51	AQU
24	5:32	PIS
26	10:25	ARI
28	11:49	TAU
30	11:14	GEM

DEC
2	10:44	CAN
4	12:20	LEO
6	17:26	VIR
9	2:21	LIB
11	14:04	SCO
14	2:53	SAG
16	15:21	CAP
19	2:29	AQU
21	11:28	PIS
23	17:41	ARI
25	20:57	TAU
27	21:58	GEM
29	22:07	CAN
31	23:09	LEO

— 107 —

LOVE SIGNS FOR BEGINNERS

—1965—

JAN
1	20:06	CAP
4	9:04	AQU
6	21:06	PIS
9	7:08	ARI
11	14:10	TAU
13	17:48	GEM
15	18:35	CAN
17	17:57	LEO
19	17:55	VIR
21	20:28	LIB
24	3:01	SCO
26	13:32	SAG
29	2:21	CAP
31	15:18	AQU

FEB
3	2:56	PIS
5	12:43	ARI
7	19:35	TAU
10	1:36	GEM
12	4:14	CAN
14	4:54	LEO
16	5:05	VIR
18	6:45	LIB
20	11:45	SCO
22	20:57	SAG
25	9:17	CAP
27	22:14	AQU

MAR
2	9:38	PIS
4	18:45	ARI
7	1:49	TAU
9	7:14	GEM
11	11:03	CAN
13	13:23	LEOP
15	14:55	VIR
17	17:04	LIB
19	21:32	SCO
22	5:37	SAG
24	17:07	CAP
27	5:59	AQU
29	17:32	PIS

APR
3	2:19	ARI
5	8:29	TAU
7	12:55	GEM
9	16:24	CAN
11	19:24	LEO
14	22:14	VIR
16	1:38	LIB
18	6:42	SCO
20	14:31	SAG
23	1:24	CAP
25	14:04	AQU
28	2:02	PIS
30	11:12	ARI
—	17:04	TAU

MAY
2	20:26	GEM
4	22:39	CAN
7	0:50	LEO
9	3:47	VIR
11	8:04	LIB
13	14:10	SCO
15	22:32	SAG
18	9:20	CAP
20	21:50	AQU
23	10:14	PIS
25	20:19	ARI
28	2:48	TAU
30	5:58	GEM

JUN
1	7:05	CAN
3	7:46	LEO
5	9:33	VIR
7	13:29	LIB
9	20:04	SCO
12	5:10	SAG
14	16:20	CAP
17	4:51	AQU
19	17:29	PIS
22	4:29	ARI
24	12:16	TAU
26	16:18	GEM
28	17:20	CAN
30	16:59	LEO

JUL
2	17:11	VIR
4	19:43	LIB
7	1:38	SCO
9	10:53	SAG
11	22:29	CAP
14	11:08	AQU
16	23:45	PIS
19	11:13	ARI
21	20:14	TAU
24	3:53	GEM
26	3:37	CAN
28	2:55	LEO
30	—	VIR

AUG
3	3:54	LIB
5	8:20	SCO
7	16:49	SAG
10	4:22	CAP
12	17:09	AQU
15	5:37	PIS
17	16:57	ARI
20	2:27	TAU
22	9:20	GEM
24	13:04	CAN
26	14:01	LEO
28	13:52	VIR
30	16:54	LIB

SEP
1	24:00	SAG
4	10:51	CAP
6	23:34	AQU
9	11:57	PIS
11	7:56	ARI
14	16:16	TAU
16	20:40	GEM
18	4:51	CAN
20	7:13	LEO
22	9:21	VIR
24	12:31	LIB
26	18:09	SCO
29	3:05	SAG
31	14:49	CAP

OCT
1	18:29	CAP
4	6:48	AQU
6	19:14	PIS
9	5:54	ARI
11	14:16	TAU
13	20:40	GEM
16	1:27	CAN
18	15:06	LEO
20	20:01	VIR
22	4:51	LIB
24	9:21	SCO
27	12:31	SAG
29	18:09	CAP
31	—	AQU

NOV
3	3:23	PIS
5	14:21	ARI
7	22:29	TAU
10	3:54	GEM
12	10:13	CAN
15	16:10	LEO
18	2:56	VIR
20	—	LIB
22	11:45	SCO
25	23:03	SAG
27	11:40	CAP

DEC
2	23:22	PIS
5	8:11	ARI
7	13:27	TAU
9	15:57	GEM
12	17:08	CAN
14	18:35	LEO
16	21:33	VIR
19	2:40	LIB
21	10:01	SCO
23	19:27	SAG
25	6:44	CAP
27	19:17	AQU
30	7:40	PIS

—1964—

JAN
3	2:48	VIR
5	10:10	LIB
7	21:04	SCO
10	9:49	SAG
12	22:14	CAP
15	8:48	AQU
17	17:04	PIS
19	23:10	ARI
22	3:23	TAU
24	6:05	GEM
26	7:51	CAN
28	9:45	LEO
30	13:09	VIR

FEB
1	19:25	LIB
4	5:12	SCO
6	17:35	SAG
9	6:11	CAP
11	16:39	AQU
14	0:09	PIS
16	5:10	ARI
18	8:45	TAU
20	11:48	GEM
22	14:49	CAN
24	18:11	LEO
26	22:30	VIR
29	4:46	LIB

MAR
2	13:54	SCO
5	1:47	SAG
7	14:35	CAP
10	1:36	AQU
12	9:05	PIS
14	13:15	ARI
16	15:30	TAU
18	17:26	GEM
20	20:11	CAN
23	0:15	LEO
25	5:42	VIR
27	12:48	LIB
29	22:03	SCO

APR
1	9:41	SAG
3	22:36	CAP
6	10:24	AQU
8	18:47	PIS
10	23:08	ARI
13	0:37	TAU
15	1:06	GEM
17	2:23	CAN
19	5:40	LEO
21	11:17	VIR
23	19:08	LIB
26	5:01	SCO
28	16:46	SAG

MAY
1	5:42	CAP
3	18:06	AQU
6	3:43	PIS
8	9:16	ARI
10	11:09	TAU
12	11:01	GEM
14	10:53	CAN
16	12:31	LEO
18	17:02	VIR
21	0:41	LIB
23	10:58	SCO
25	23:03	SAG
28	12:00	CAP
31	0:32	AQU

JUN
2	11:01	PIS
4	18:03	ARI
6	21:20	TAU
8	21:50	GEM
10	21:16	CAN
12	21:35	LEO
15	0:27	VIR
17	6:54	LIB
19	16:49	SCO
22	5:03	SAG
24	18:02	CAP
27	6:22	AQU
29	16:56	PIS

JUL
2	0:52	ARI
4	5:42	TAU
6	7:57	GEM
8	8:01	CAN
10	7:31	LEO
12	9:44	VIR
14	14:41	LIB
16	23:32	SCO
19	11:28	SAG
22	0:27	CAP
24	12:30	AQU
26	22:16	PIS
29	6:25	ARI
31	12:00	TAU

AUG
2	15:28	GEM
4	17:13	CAN
6	18:11	LEO
8	19:50	VIR
10	23:51	LIB
13	7:31	SCO
15	18:44	SAG
18	7:38	CAP
20	19:39	AQU
23	5:13	PIS
25	12:15	ARI
27	17:24	TAU
29	21:16	GEM

SEP
1	0:13	CAN
3	2:36	LEO
5	5:12	VIR
7	9:19	LIB
9	16:19	SCO
12	2:47	SAG
14	15:30	CAP
17	3:47	AQU
19	13:22	PIS
21	19:44	ARI
23	23:46	TAU
26	2:46	GEM
28	5:39	CAN
30	8:53	LEO

OCT
2	12:42	VIR
4	17:44	LIB
7	0:57	SCO
9	11:02	SAG
11	23:32	CAP
14	12:15	AQU
16	22:33	PIS
19	5:05	ARI
21	10:03	TAU
23	11:37	GEM
25	14:14	CAN
27	18:25	LEO

NOV
1	0:24	LIB
3	8:25	SCO
5	18:43	SAG
8	7:06	CAP
10	20:08	AQU
13	7:28	PIS
15	15:10	ARI
17	18:57	TAU
19	20:04	GEM
21	20:59	CAN
23	—	LEO
26	0:02	VIR
28	5:54	LIB
30	14:31	SCO

DEC
3	1:24	SAG
5	13:53	CAP
8	2:57	AQU
10	15:00	PIS
13	0:12	ARI
15	5:33	TAU
17	7:02	GEM
19	7:02	CAN
21	6:31	LEO
23	7:41	VIR
25	12:04	LIB
27	20:11	SCO
30	7:20	SAG

LOVE SIGNS FOR BEGINNERS

—1966—

JAN
1	17:46	TAU	
4	0:06	GEM	
6	2:40	CAN	
8	2:50	LEO	
10	2:34	VIR	
12	3:53	LIB	
14	8:08	SCO	
16	15:39	SAG	
19	1:45	CAP	
21	13:26	AQU	
24	1:58	PIS	
26	14:33	ARI	
29	1:43	TAU	
31	9:43	GEM	

FEB
2	13:41	LIB	
4	14:14	SCO	
6	13:11	SAG	
8	12:50	CAP	
10	15:15	AQU	
12	21:33	PIS	
15	7:26	ARI	
17	19:26	TAU	
20	8:08	GEM	
22	20:30	CAN	
25	7:53	LEO	
27	17:03	VIR	

MAR
2	22:48	CAN	
4	0:57	LEO	
6	0:36	VIR	
7	23:48	LIB	
10	0:47	SCO	
12	5:18	SAG	
14	13:55	CAP	
17	1:35	AQU	
19	14:19	PIS	
22	2:33	ARI	
24	13:32	TAU	
26	22:41	GEM	
29	5:23	CAN	
31	9:12	LEO	

APR
2	10:31	VIR	
4	10:39	LIB	
6	11:30	SCO	
8	14:54	SAG	
10	22:02	CAP	
13	8:42	AQU	
15	21:13	PIS	
18	9:27	ARI	
20	20:00	TAU	
23	10:48	GEM	
25	15:09	CAN	
27	17:50	LEO	
29		VIR	

MAY
1	19:31	ARI	
3	21:23	TAU	
6	0:52	GEM	
8	7:12	CAN	
10	16:52	LEO	
13	4:55	VIR	
15	17:15	LIB	
18	3:49	SCO	
20	11:40	SAG	
22	17:00	CAP	
24	20:37	AQU	
26	23:22	PIS	
29	2:00	ARI	
31	5:11	TAU	

JUN
2	9:38	SAG	
4	16:10	CAP	
7	1:21	AQU	
9	12:57	PIS	
12	1:26	ARI	
14	12:30	TAU	
16	20:26	GEM	
19	1:17	CAN	
21	3:08	LEO	
23	5:09	VIR	
25	7:23	LIB	
27	11:04	SCO	
29	16:31	SAG	

JUL
2	23:51	CAP	
5	9:14	AQU	
7	20:39	PIS	
10	9:16	ARI	
12	21:03	TAU	
15	5:51	GEM	
17	10:44	CAN	
19	12:27	LEO	
21	12:46	VIR	
23	13:38	LIB	
25	16:32	SCO	
27	22:04	SAG	
30	6:04	CAP	

AUG
3	3:36	PIS	
5	16:15	ARI	
8	4:38	TAU	
10	14:38	GEM	
12	20:42	CAN	
14	22:50	LEO	
16	22:35	VIR	
18	22:05	LIB	
20	23:24	SCO	
23	3:51	SAG	
25	11:37	CAP	
27	21:56	AQU	
30	9:48	PIS	

SEP
1	22:27	ARI	
4	10:59	TAU	
6	21:52	GEM	
9	5:26	CAN	
11	9:01	LEO	
13	9:26	VIR	
15	8:33	LIB	
17	8:34	SCO	
19	11:21	SAG	
21	17:52	CAP	
24	3:48	AQU	
26	15:45	PIS	
29	4:29	ARI	

OCT
1	16:47	TAU	
4	3:43	GEM	
6	12:12	CAN	
8	17:25	LEO	
10	19:27	VIR	
12	19:29	LIB	
14	19:21	SCO	
16	20:59	SAG	
19	1:55	CAP	
21	10:41	AQU	
23	22:20	PIS	
26	11:03	ARI	
28	23:05	TAU	
31	9:28	GEM	

NOV
2	17:43	CAN	
4	23:36	LEO	
7	3:10	VIR	
9	4:54	LIB	
11	5:53	SCO	
13	7:36	SAG	
15	11:37	CAP	
17	19:03	AQU	
20	5:53	PIS	
22	18:31	ARI	
25	6:37	TAU	
27	16:31	GEM	
29	23:50	CAN	

DEC
2	5:02	LEO	
4	8:48	VIR	
6	11:43	LIB	
8	14:18	SCO	
10	17:13	SAG	
12	21:30	CAP	
15	4:19	AQU	
17	14:17	PIS	
20	2:39	ARI	
22	15:07	TAU	
25	1:14	GEM	
27	7:58	CAN	
29	11:57	LEO	
31	14:33	VIR	

—1967—

JAN
2	17:04	LIB	
4	20:16	SCO	
7	0:28	SAG	
9	5:53	CAP	
11	13:05	AQU	
13	22:45	PIS	
16	10:48	ARI	
18	23:39	TAU	
21	10:38	GEM	
23	17:51	CAN	
25	21:20	LEO	
27	22:36	VIR	
29	23:33	LIB	

FEB
1	1:44	SCO	
3	5:55	SAG	
5	12:10	CAP	
7	20:17	AQU	
10	6:19	PIS	
12	18:17	ARI	
15	7:19	TAU	
17	19:16	GEM	
20	3:48	CAN	
22	7:51	LEO	
24	9:04	VIR	
26	8:44	LIB	
28	9:09	SCO	

MAR
2	11:53	SAG	
4	17:35	CAP	
7	2:03	AQU	
9	12:41	PIS	
12	0:53	ARI	
14	13:54	TAU	
17	2:19	GEM	
19	12:10	CAN	
21	18:04	LEO	
23	20:08	VIR	
25	19:50	LIB	
27	19:10	SCO	
29	20:08	SAG	

APR
1	0:11	CAP	
3	7:49	AQU	
5	18:29	PIS	
8	6:57	ARI	
10	19:56	TAU	
13	8:15	GEM	
15	18:37	CAN	
18	1:54	LEO	
20	5:43	VIR	
22	6:19	LIB	
24	6:27	SCO	
26	6:54	SAG	
28	8:54	CAP	
30	14:57	AQU	

MAY
3	0:47	PIS	
5	13:10	ARI	
8	2:09	TAU	
10	14:08	GEM	
13	0:11	CAN	
15	7:49	LEO	
17	12:52	VIR	
19	15:31	LIB	
21	16:30	SCO	
23	17:06	SAG	
25	18:58	CAP	
27	23:44	AQU	
30	8:18	PIS	

JUN
1	20:07	ARI	
4	9:04	TAU	
6	20:52	GEM	
9	6:18	CAN	
11	13:19	LEO	
13	18:24	VIR	
15	21:58	LIB	
18	0:25	SCO	
20	2:40	SAG	
22	4:46	CAP	
24	9:11	AQU	
26	16:49	PIS	
29	3:53	ARI	

JUL
1	16:43	ARI	
4	4:39	TAU	
6	13:47	GEM	
8	19:58	CAN	
11	0:07	LEO	
13	3:20	VIR	
15	6:17	LIB	
17	9:22	SCO	
19	12:59	SAG	
21	17:59	CAP	
24	1:28	AQU	
26	12:00	PIS	
29	0:40	ARI	
31	13:00	TAU	

AUG
3	22:32	CAN	
5	4:26	LEO	
7	7:36	VIR	
9	9:34	LIB	
11	11:44	SCO	
13	14:52	SAG	
15	19:16	CAP	
18	1:17	AQU	
20	9:18	PIS	
22	19:47	ARI	
25	8:21	TAU	
27	20:50	GEM	
30	7:34	CAN	

SEP
1	14:08	LEO	
3	17:07	VIR	
5	18:03	LIB	
7	18:44	SCO	
9	20:40	SAG	
12	0:43	CAP	
14	7:08	AQU	
16	15:53	PIS	
19	2:46	ARI	
21	15:20	TAU	
24	4:21	GEM	
26	15:45	CAN	
28	23:41	LEO	

OCT
1	3:38	VIR	
3	4:34	LIB	
5	4:14	SCO	
7	4:32	SAG	
9	7:04	CAP	
11	12:45	AQU	
13	21:38	PIS	
16	8:58	ARI	
18	21:41	TAU	
21	10:38	GEM	
23	22:27	CAN	
26	7:40	LEO	
28	13:19	VIR	
30	15:31	LIB	

NOV
1	15:26	SCO	
3	14:51	SAG	
5	15:44	CAP	
7	19:45	AQU	
10	3:42	PIS	
12	14:58	ARI	
15	3:52	TAU	
17	16:40	GEM	
20	4:13	CAN	
22	13:47	LEO	
24	20:46	VIR	
27	0:48	LIB	
29	2:13	SCO	

DEC
1	2:10	SAG	
3	2:25	CAP	
5	4:57	AQU	
7	11:19	PIS	
9	21:43	ARI	
12	10:32	TAU	
14	23:18	GEM	
17	10:23	CAN	
19	19:21	LEO	
22	2:21	VIR	
24	7:27	LIB	
26	10:36	SCO	
28	12:09	SAG	
30	13:11	CAP	

— 109 —

LOVE SIGNS FOR BEGINNERS

—1968—

JAN			FEB			MAR			APR		
1	15:23	AQU	2	14:39	ARI	3	10:27	TAU	2	6:40	GEM
3	20:35	PIS	5	2:15	TAU	6	23:17	GEM	4	19:13	CAN
6	5:45	ARI	7	15:09	GEM	8	11:21	CAN	7	5:28	LEO
8	18:02	TAU	10	2:34	CAN	10	20:27	LEO	9	12:04	VIR
11	6:54	GEM	12	10:50	LEO	13	1:51	VIR	11	15:32	LIB
13	17:54	CAN	14	16:02	VIR	15	4:23	LIB	13	15:32	SCO
16	2:09	LEO	16	19:21	LIB	17	5:33	SCO	15	16:23	SAG
18	8:11	VIR	18	21:48	SCO	19	6:53	SAG	17	19:57	CAP
20	12:47	LIB	21	0:48	SAG	21	9:34	CAP	20	2:46	AQU
22	16:28	SCO	23	4:12	CAP	23	14:16	AQU	22	12:32	PIS
24	19:23	SAG	25	8:37	AQU	25	21:15	PIS	25	0:22	ARI
26	21:57	CAP	27	14:42	PIS	28	6:32	ARI	27	13:11	TAU
29	1:06	AQU	29	23:14	ARI	30	17:55	TAU			
31	6:16	PIS									

MAY			JUN			JUL			AUG		
2	1:50	GEM	3	3:52	VIR	2	16:10	LIB	3	2:11	SCO
4	12:54	CAN	5	9:49	LIB	4	20:20	SCO	5	5:11	SAG
6	20:58	LEO	7	12:30	SCO	6	22:05	SAG	7	6:57	CAP
9	1:21	VIR	9	12:42	SAG	8	22:24	CAP	9	8:37	AQU
11	2:30	LIB	11	12:05	CAP	10	23:03	AQU	11	11:45	PIS
13	1:53	SCO	13	12:46	AQU	13	1:55	PIS	13	17:53	ARI
15	1:31	SAG	15	16:42	PIS	15	8:51	ARI	16	3:36	TAU
17	3:22	CAP	18	0:50	ARI	17	19:30	TAU	18	15:51	GEM
19	8:53	AQU	20	12:25	TAU	20	8:13	GEM	21	4:15	CAN
21	18:14	PIS	23	1:22	GEM	22	20:31	CAN	23	14:40	LEO
24	6:15	ARI	25	13:43	CAN	25	7:22	LEO	25	22:21	VIR
26	19:12	TAU	27	23:30	LEO	27	15:10	VIR	28	3:45	LIB
29	7:43	GEM	30	9:26	VIR	29	21:32	LIB	30	7:38	SCO
31	18:53	CAN								10:40	SAG

SEP			OCT			NOV			DEC		
1	13:22	CAP	3	16:19	PIS	1	16:51	ARI	3	8:58	GEM
3	16:19	AQU	5	20:27	ARI	4	3:01	TAU	6	21:06	CAN
5	20:27	PIS	8	2:49	TAU	6	14:48	GEM	9	9:43	LEO
8	2:49	ARI	10	12:06	GEM	9	3:26	CAN	11	22:02	VIR
10	12:06	TAU	12	23:54	CAN	11	15:45	LEO	14	8:59	LIB
13	1:53	GEM	15	12:28	LEO	14	1:55	VIR	16	17:08	SCO
15	13:51	CAN	17	23:05	VIR	16	8:26	LIB	18	21:31	SAG
18	3:22	LEO	20	0:05	LIB	18	11:04	SCO	20	22:28	CAP
20	8:53	VIR	22	0:32	SCO	20	11:02	SAG	22	21:32	AQU
22	14:16	LIB	24	1:13	SAG	22	10:19	CAP	24	20:59	PIS
24	18:14	SCO	26	3:43	CAP	24	11:02	AQU	26	23:01	ARI
26	19:12	SAG	28	8:54	AQU	26	14:52	PIS	29	5:02	TAU
28	19:23	CAP	30	22:11	PIS	28	22:26	ARI	31	14:57	GEM
30	22:11	AQU								3:11	CAN

—1969—

JAN			FEB			MAR			APR		
2	15:53	CAN	1	10:29	LEO	3	4:07	VIR	1	20:03	LIB
5	3:55	LEO	3	20:40	VIR	5	11:34	LIB	4	0:22	SCO
7	14:42	VIR	6	5:00	LIB	7	16:56	SCO	6	2:57	SAG
9	23:32	LIB	8	11:18	SCO	9	20:48	SAG	8	5:04	CAP
12	5:32	SCO	10	15:23	SAG	11	23:40	CAP	10	7:46	AQU
14	8:19	SAG	12	17:28	CAP	14	2:09	AQU	12	11:41	PIS
16	8:39	CAP	14	18:30	AQU	16	5:04	PIS	14	17:13	ARI
18	8:17	AQU	16	20:03	PIS	18	9:27	ARI	17	0:43	TAU
20	9:20	PIS	18	23:48	ARI	20	16:20	TAU	19	10:28	GEM
22	13:43	ARI	21	7:02	TAU	23	2:12	GEM	21	22:17	CAN
24	22:13	TAU	23	17:41	GEM	25	14:18	CAN	24	10:51	LEO
27	9:53	GEM	26	6:11	CAN	28	2:37	LEO	26	21:57	VIR
29	22:36	CAN	28	18:12	LEO	30	12:54	VIR	29	5:44	LIB

MAY			JUN			JUL			AUG		
1	9:50	SCO	1	21:07	CAP	1	6:49	AQU	1	19:54	ARI
3	11:19	SAG	3	21:03	AQU	3	7:26	PIS	4	2:02	TAU
5	11:57	CAP	5	23:13	PIS	5	11:16	ARI	6	11:49	GEM
7	13:28	AQU	8	4:36	ARI	7	18:53	TAU	8	23:57	CAN
9	17:04	PIS	10	13:06	TAU	10	5:31	GEM	11	12:38	LEO
11	23:09	ARI	12	23:48	GEM	12	17:47	CAN	14	0:32	VIR
14	7:28	TAU	15	11:52	CAN	15	6:29	LEO	16	10:51	LIB
16	17:41	GEM	18	0:35	LEO	17	18:42	VIR	18	18:54	SCO
19	5:30	CAN	20	12:53	VIR	20	5:20	LIB	21	0:12	SAG
21	18:12	LEO	22	23:05	LIB	22	13:04	SCO	23	2:49	CAP
24	6:07	VIR	25	5:31	SCO	24	17:10	SAG	25	3:36	AQU
26	15:07	LIB	27	8:00	SAG	26	18:09	CAP	27	4:03	PIS
28	20:05	SCO	29	7:44	CAP	28	17:30	AQU	29	5:57	ARI
30	21:30	SAG				30	17:30	PIS	31	10:50	TAU

SEP			OCT			NOV			DEC		
2	19:23	GEM	2	14:52	CAN	1	11:35	LEO	3	8:14	VIR
5	6:57	CAN	5	3:25	LEO	4	0:00	VIR	5	19:17	LIB
7	19:36	LEO	7	15:21	VIR	6	9:59	LIB	8	2:30	SCO
10	7:20	VIR	10	0:48	LIB	8	16:18	SCO	10	5:43	SAG
12	17:01	LIB	12	7:19	SCO	10	19:30	SAG	12	6:20	CAP
15	0:25	SCO	14	11:33	SAG	12	21:08	CAP	14	6:27	AQU
17	5:42	SAG	16	14:35	CAP	14	22:53	AQU	16	7:56	PIS
19	9:14	CAP	18	17:21	AQU	17	1:52	PIS	18	11:56	ARI
21	11:31	AQU	20	20:26	PIS	19	6:32	ARI	20	18:35	TAU
23	13:22	PIS	23	0:17	ARI	21	12:52	TAU	23	3:28	GEM
25	15:55	ARI	25	5:32	TAU	23	20:59	GEM	25	14:08	CAN
27	20:29	TAU	27	13:00	GEM	26	7:10	CAN	28	2:21	LEO
30	4:05	GEM	29	23:13	CAN	28	19:22	LEO	30	15:20	VIR
										3:18	LIB

— 110 —

–1970–

JAN			FEB			MAR			APR		
2	12:03	SCO	1	1:50	SAG	2	12:54	CAP	3	0:01	PIS
4	16:33	SAG	3	4:22	CAP	4	14:34	AQU	5	1:32	ARI
6	17:30	CAP	5	4:19	AQU	6	14:49	PIS	7	4:02	TAU
8	16:47	AQU	7	3:37	PIS	8	15:16	ARI	9	9:02	GEM
10	16:36	PIS	9	4:17	ARI	10	17:43	TAU	11	17:33	CAN
12	18:48	ARI	11	7:59	TAU	12	23:37	GEM	14	5:16	LEO
15	0:20	TAU	13	15:29	GEM	15	9:18	CAN	16	18:07	VIR
17	9:07	GEM	16	2:17	CAN	17	21:40	LEO	19	5:35	LIB
19	20:13	CAN	18	14:53	LEO	20	10:30	VIR	21	14:15	SCO
22	8:40	LEO	21	3:42	VIR	22	21:57	LIB	23	20:15	SAG
24	21:33	VIR	23	15:30	LIB	25	7:10	SCO	26	0:26	CAP
27	9:42	LIB	26	1:23	SCO	27	14:07	SAG	28	3:43	AQU
29	19:34	SCO	28	8:38	SAG	29	19:00	CAP	30	6:37	PIS
						31	22:08	AQU			

MAY			JUN			JUL			AUG		
2	9:32	ARI	3	2:10	GEM	2	17:21	CAN	1	10:44	LEO
4	13:05	TAU	5	10:25	CAN	5	4:26	LEO	3	23:34	VIR
6	18:17	GEM	7	21:17	LEO	7	17:11	VIR	6	12:32	LIB
9	2:17	CAN	10	10:02	VIR	10	6:02	LIB	8	23:57	SCO
11	13:22	LEO	12	22:28	LIB	12	16:41	SCO	11	8:07	SAG
14	2:10	VIR	15	8:02	SCO	14	23:26	SAG	13	12:25	CAP
16	14:02	LIB	17	13:39	SAG	17	2:19	CAP	15	13:31	AQU
18	22:49	SCO	19	16:05	CAP	19	2:44	AQU	17	13:01	PIS
21	4:11	SAG	21	17:00	AQU	21	2:36	PIS	19	12:50	QRI
23	7:13	CAP	23	18:11	PIS	23	3:42	ARI	21	14:46	TAU
25	9:25	AQU	25	20:52	ARI	25	7:18	TAU	23	20:03	GEM
27	11:59	PIS	28	1:35	TAU	27	13:53	GEM	26	4:58	CAN
29	15:27	ARI	30	8:24	GEM	29	23:14	CAN	28	16:38	LEO
31	20:03	TAU							31	5:36	VIR

SEP			OCT			NOV			DEC		
2	18:25	LIB	2	11:35	SCO	1	2:24	SAG	2	18:45	AQU
5	5:54	SCO	4	20:31	SAG	3	8:32	CAP	4	21:55	PIS
7	14:58	SAG	7	3:10	CAP	5	13:11	AQU	7	1:03	ARI
9	20:51	CAP	9	7:26	AQU	7	16:33	PIS	9	4:24	TAU
11	23:34	AQU	11	9:30	PIS	9	18:52	ARI	11	8:33	GEM
13	23:57	PIS	13	10:12	ARI	11	20:50	TAU	13	14:32	CAN
15	23:35	ARI	15	11:00	TAU	13	23:48	GEM	15	23:21	LEO
18	0:21	TAU	17	13:43	GEM	16	5:23	CAN	18	11:04	VIR
20	4:02	GEM	19	19:59	CAN	18	14:36	LEO	21	0:01	LIB
22	11:41	CAN	22	6:12	LEO	21	2:50	VIR	23	11:27	SCO
24	22:54	LEO	24	18:57	VIR	23	15:39	LIB	25	19:28	SAG
27	11:53	VIR	27	7:37	LIB	26	2:25	SCO	28	0:01	CAP
30	0:33	LIB	29	18:15	SCO	28	10:02	SAG	30	2:24	AQU
						30	15:06	CAP			

–1971–

JAN			FEB			MAR			APR		
1	4:08	PIS	1	15:48	TAU	3	3:01	GEM	1	16:51	CAN
3	6:26	ARI	3	20:34	GEM	5	9:47	CAN	4	2:05	LEO
5	10:00	TAU	6	4:07	CAN	7	19:55	LEO	6	14:16	VIR
7	15:08	GEM	8	14:06	LEO	10	8:10	VIR	9	3:17	LIB
9	22:09	CAN	11	1:58	VIR	12	21:06	LIB	11	15:28	SCO
12	7:24	LEO	13	14:50	LIB	15	9:31	SCO	14	2:03	SAG
14	18:57	VIR	16	3:22	SCO	17	20:23	SAG	16	10:38	CAP
17	7:53	LIB	18	13:45	SAG	20	4:37	CAP	18	16:46	AQU
19	20:04	SCO	20	20:37	CAP	22	9:29	AQU	20	20:08	PIS
22	5:16	SAG	22	23:43	AQU	24	11:07	PIS	22	21:08	ARI
24	10:33	CAP	25	0:05	PIS	26	10:45	ARI	24	21:06	TAU
26	12:36	AQU	26	23:30	ARI	28	10:15	TAU	26	21:58	GEM
28	13:01	PIS	28	23:54	TAU	30	11:43	GEM	29	1:43	CAN
30	13:36	ARI									

MAY			JUN			JUL			AUG		
1	9:34	LEO	2	17:26	LIB	2	13:46	SCO	1	8:49	SAG
3	21:03	VIR	5	5:36	SCO	4	23:59	SAG	3	16:32	CAP
6	9:59	LIB	7	15:28	SAG	7	7:03	CAP	5	20:47	AQU
8	22:03	SCO	9	22:45	CAP	9	11:26	AQU	7	22:34	PIS
11	8:08	SAG	12	4:03	AQU	11	14:14	PIS	9	23:27	ARI
13	16:09	CAP	14	8:01	PIS	13	16:32	ARI	12	0:55	TAU
15	22:19	AQU	16	11:06	ARI	15	19:10	TAU	14	4:10	GEM
18	2:39	PIS	18	13:39	TAU	17	22:47	GEM	16	9:50	CAN
20	5:11	ARI	20	16:24	GEM	20	3:56	CAN	18	17:57	LEO
22	6:31	TAU	22	20:30	CAN	22	11:16	LEO	21	4:19	VIR
24	8:01	GEM	25	3:12	LEO	24	21:09	VIR	23	16:22	LIB
26	11:26	CAN	27	13:06	VIR	27	9:12	LIB	26	5:09	SCO
28	18:16	LEO	30	1:22	LIB	29	21:50	SCO	28	16:56	SAG
31	4:48	VIR							31	1:54	CAP

SEP			OCT			NOV			DEC		
2	7:04	AQU	1	19:37	PIS	2	5:55	TAU	1	16:25	GEM
4	8:51	PIS	3	19:40	ARI	4	5:27	GEM	3	17:51	CAN
6	8:43	ARI	5	18:42	TAU	6	7:15	CAN	5	22:17	LEO
8	8:37	TAU	7	18:53	GEM	8	12:56	LEO	8	6:40	VIR
10	10:25	GEM	9	22:10	CAN	10	22:44	VIR	10	18:19	LIB
12	15:21	CAN	12	5:30	LEO	13	11:05	LIB	13	7:01	SCO
14	23:38	LEO	14	16:16	VIR	15	23:49	SCO	15	18:37	SAG
17	10:29	VIR	17	4:47	LIB	18	11:30	SAG	18	4:07	CAP
19	22:47	LIB	19	17:31	SCO	20	21:36	CAP	20	11:32	AQU
22	11:33	SCO	22	5:31	SAG	23	5:52	AQU	22	17:10	PIS
24	23:43	SAG	24	16:05	CAP	25	11:48	PIS	24	21:09	ARI
27	9:53	CAP	27	0:11	AQU	27	15:04	ARI	26	23:45	TAU
29	16:39	AQU	29	4:57	PIS	29	16:08	TAU	29	1:38	GEM
			31	6:26	ARI				31	4:01	CAN

LOVE SIGNS FOR BEGINNERS

—1972—

JAN
2	8:22	LEO
5	15:50	VIR
7	22:33	LIB
9	15:03	SCO
12	2:57	SAG
14	12:26	CAP
16	19:04	AQU
18	23:28	PIS
21	2:35	ARI
23	5:17	TAU
25	8:14	GEM
27	12:01	CAN
29	17:21	LEO

FEB
1	0:56	VIR
3	11:06	LIB
5	23:18	SCO
8	11:38	SAG
10	21:50	CAP
13	4:36	AQU
15	8:11	PIS
17	9:51	ARI
19	11:11	TAU
21	13:35	GEM
23	17:52	CAN
26	0:15	LEO
28	8:39	VIR

MAR
1	19:00	LIB
4	7:00	SCO
6	19:36	SAG
9	6:49	CAP
11	18:39	AQU
13	19:27	PIS
15	19:37	ARI
17	19:37	TAU
19	21:14	GEM
21	23:26	CAN
24	5:46	LEO
26	14:48	VIR
29	1:42	LIB
31	13:48	SCO

APR
3	2:27	SAG
5	14:20	CAP
7	23:18	AQU
10	4:58	PIS
12	6:32	ARI
14	5:54	TAU
16	5:16	GEM
18	6:46	CAN
20	11:46	LEO
22	20:24	VIR
25	7:34	LIB
27	19:56	SCO
30	8:31	SAG

MAY
2	20:29	CAP
5	6:35	AQU
7	13:28	PIS
9	16:35	ARI
11	16:47	TAU
13	15:57	GEM
15	16:16	CAN
17	19:38	LEO
20	2:56	VIR
22	13:36	LIB
25	2:01	SCO
27	14:33	SAG
30	2:13	CAP

JUN
1	12:15	AQU
3	19:52	PIS
6	0:27	ARI
8	2:15	TAU
10	2:24	GEM
12	2:45	CAN
14	5:10	LEO
16	11:03	VIR
18	20:39	LIB
21	8:43	SCO
23	21:14	SAG
26	8:36	CAP
28	18:02	AQU

JUL
1	1:18	PIS
3	6:22	ARI
5	9:25	TAU
7	11:05	GEM
9	12:29	CAN
11	15:05	LEO
13	20:16	VIR
16	4:49	LIB
18	16:15	SCO
21	4:46	SAG
23	16:10	CAP
26	1:07	AQU
28	7:29	PIS
30	11:50	ARI

AUG
1	14:57	TAU
3	17:33	GEM
5	20:18	CAN
7	23:56	LEO
10	5:23	VIR
12	13:27	LIB
15	0:19	SCO
17	12:49	SAG
20	0:38	CAP
22	9:43	AQU
24	15:28	PIS
26	18:40	ARI
28	20:43	TAU
30	22:56	GEM

SEP
2	2:11	CAN
4	6:54	LEO
6	13:15	VIR
8	21:36	LIB
11	8:15	SCO
13	20:42	SAG
16	9:07	CAP
18	19:05	AQU
21	1:09	PIS
23	3:44	ARI
25	4:27	TAU
27	5:14	GEM
29	7:39	CAN

OCT
1	12:25	LEO
3	19:31	VIR
6	4:35	LIB
8	15:27	SCO
11	3:52	SAG
13	16:44	CAP
16	3:51	AQU
18	11:12	PIS
20	14:22	ARI
22	14:37	TAU
24	14:02	GEM
26	14:44	CAN
28	18:14	LEO
31	0:59	VIR

NOV
2	10:27	LIB
4	21:46	SCO
7	10:16	SAG
9	23:11	CAP
12	11:02	AQU
14	19:56	PIS
17	0:44	ARI
19	1:53	TAU
21	1:05	GEM
23	0:31	CAN
25	2:12	LEO
27	7:24	VIR
29	16:15	LIB

DEC
2	3:42	SCO
4	16:22	SAG
7	5:06	CAP
9	16:53	AQU
12	2:33	PIS
14	8:59	ARI
16	11:59	TAU
18	12:24	GEM
20	11:57	CAN
22	12:34	LEO
24	16:02	VIR
26	23:21	LIB
29	10:10	SCO
31	22:51	SAG

—1973—

JAN
3	11:30	CAP
5	22:47	AQU
8	8:03	PIS
10	14:57	ARI
12	19:24	TAU
14	21:41	GEM
16	22:39	CAN
18	23:40	LEO
21	2:23	VIR
23	8:16	LIB
25	17:52	SCO
28	6:10	SAG
30	18:54	CAP

FEB
2	5:55	AQU
4	14:22	PIS
6	20:29	ARI
9	0:53	TAU
11	4:10	GEM
13	6:44	CAN
15	9:12	LEO
17	12:31	VIR
19	17:58	LIB
22	2:35	SCO
24	14:14	SAG
27	3:04	CAP

MAR
1	14:22	AQU
3	22:31	PIS
6	3:37	ARI
8	6:51	TAU
10	9:29	GEM
12	12:29	CAN
14	16:07	LEO
16	20:42	VIR
19	2:48	LIB
21	11:15	SCO
23	22:26	SAG
26	11:16	CAP
28	23:12	AQU
31	7:55	PIS

APR
2	12:48	ARI
4	14:58	TAU
6	16:12	GEM
8	18:04	CAN
10	21:31	LEO
13	2:47	VIR
15	9:50	LIB
17	18:51	SCO
20	6:02	SAG
22	18:49	CAP
25	7:21	AQU
27	17:10	PIS
29	22:53	ARI

MAY
2	1:01	TAU
4	1:16	GEM
6	1:35	CAN
8	3:36	LEO
10	8:13	VIR
12	15:31	LIB
15	1:09	SCO
17	12:41	SAG
20	1:30	CAP
22	14:17	AQU
25	1:05	PIS
27	8:14	ARI
29	11:28	TAU
31	11:53	GEM

JUN
2	11:21	CAN
4	11:49	LEO
6	14:51	VIR
8	21:16	LIB
11	6:52	SCO
13	18:43	SAG
16	7:37	CAP
18	20:19	AQU
21	7:29	PIS
23	15:48	ARI
25	20:37	TAU
27	22:18	GEM
29	22:08	CAN

JUL
1	21:55	LEO
3	23:31	VIR
6	4:23	LIB
8	13:05	SCO
11	0:48	SAG
13	13:45	CAP
16	1:58	AQU
18	13:07	PIS
20	21:43	ARI
23	3:41	TAU
25	6:58	GEM
27	8:10	CAN
29	8:29	LEO
31	9:34	VIR

AUG
2	13:12	LIB
4	20:35	SCO
7	7:37	SAG
9	20:30	CAP
12	8:52	AQU
14	19:14	PIS
17	3:16	ARI
19	9:14	TAU
21	13:26	GEM
23	16:08	CAN
25	17:49	LEO
27	19:33	VIR
29	22:52	LIB

SEP
1	5:17	SCO
3	15:24	SAG
6	4:01	CAP
8	16:30	AQU
11	2:40	PIS
13	9:56	ARI
15	14:59	TAU
17	18:48	GEM
19	22:01	CAN
22	0:56	LEO
24	3:58	VIR
26	8:00	LIB
28	14:18	SCO
30	23:47	SAG

OCT
3	12:02	CAP
6	0:49	AQU
8	11:23	PIS
10	18:29	ARI
12	22:36	TAU
15	1:09	GEM
17	3:28	CAN
19	6:25	LEO
21	10:19	VIR
23	15:28	LIB
25	22:28	SCO
28	7:57	SAG
30	19:57	CAP

NOV
2	8:58	AQU
4	20:26	PIS
7	4:19	ARI
9	8:25	TAU
11	9:59	GEM
13	10:46	CAN
15	12:20	LEO
17	15:41	VIR
19	21:20	LIB
22	5:06	SCO
24	15:11	SAG
27	3:13	CAP
29	16:17	AQU

DEC
2	4:32	PIS
4	13:50	ARI
6	19:08	TAU
8	20:58	GEM
10	20:52	CAN
12	20:44	LEO
14	22:20	VIR
17	2:53	LIB
19	10:44	SCO
21	21:20	SAG
24	9:41	CAP
26	22:43	AQU
29	11:10	PIS
31	21:34	ARI

— 112 —

—1974—

JAN
Day	Time	Sign
3	4:38	TAU
5	8:00	GEM
7	8:28	CAN
9	7:42	LEO
11	7:41	VIR
13	10:21	LIB
15	16:54	SCO
18	3:12	SAG
20	15:47	CAP
23	4:50	AQU
25	17:00	PIS
28	3:32	ARI
30	11:41	TAU

FEB
Day	Time	Sign
1	16:53	GEM
3	19:06	CAN
5	19:12	LEO
7	18:52	VIR
9	20:10	LIB
12	0:58	SCO
14	10:01	SAG
16	22:16	CAP
19	11:21	AQU
21	23:15	PIS
24	9:12	ARI
26	17:11	TAU
28	23:10	GEM

MAR
Day	Time	Sign
3	3:00	CAN
5	4:49	LEO
7	5:33	VIR
9	6:52	LIB
11	10:40	SCO
13	18:20	SAG
16	5:41	CAP
18	18:38	AQU
21	6:33	PIS
23	16:02	ARI
25	23:09	TAU
28	4:33	GEM
30	8:40	CAN

APR
Day	Time	Sign
1	11:41	LEO
3	13:56	VIR
5	16:22	LIB
7	20:25	SCO
10	3:27	SAG
12	13:56	CAP
15	2:34	AQU
17	14:44	PIS
20	0:20	ARI
22	6:53	TAU
24	11:11	GEM
26	14:17	CAN
28	17:03	LEO
30	20:00	VIR

MAY
Day	Time	Sign
3	23:39	LIB
5	4:43	SCO
7	12:05	SAG
9	22:15	CAP
12	10:34	AQU
14	23:03	PIS
17	9:20	ARI
19	16:10	TAU
21	19:54	GEM
23	21:46	CAN
25	23:12	LEO
28	1:25	VIR
30	5:16	LIB

JUN
Day	Time	Sign
1	11:10	SCO
3	19:21	SAG
6	5:48	CAP
8	18:02	AQU
11	6:43	PIS
13	17:52	ARI
16	1:46	TAU
18	5:59	GEM
20	7:21	CAN
22	7:30	LEO
24	8:11	VIR
26	10:57	LIB
28	16:40	SCO

JUL
Day	Time	Sign
1	1:20	SAG
3	12:19	CAP
6	0:41	AQU
8	13:25	PIS
11	1:10	ARI
13	10:21	TAU
15	15:54	GEM
17	17:56	CAN
19	17:43	LEO
21	17:10	VIR
23	18:19	LIB
25	22:45	SCO
28	7:00	SAG
30	18:11	CAP

AUG
Day	Time	Sign
2	6:46	AQU
4	19:26	PIS
7	7:15	ARI
9	17:13	TAU
12	0:15	GEM
14	3:49	CAN
16	4:26	LEO
18	3:45	VIR
20	3:42	LIB
22	6:37	SCO
24	13:34	SAG
27	0:15	CAP
29	12:53	AQU

SEP
Day	Time	Sign
3	1:29	PIS
5	12:58	ARI
7	22:50	TAU
10	6:36	GEM
12	11:40	CAN
14	13:54	LEO
16	14:12	VIR
18	14:17	LIB
20	16:14	SCO
22	21:46	SAG
25	7:22	CAP
27	19:38	AQU
30	8:14	PIS

OCT
Day	Time	Sign
3	4:39	ARI
5	12:00	TAU
7	17:30	GEM
9	21:03	CAN
11	22:56	LEO
14	0:11	VIR
16	2:23	LIB
18	7:14	SCO
20	15:44	SAG
23	3:20	CAP
25	15:57	AQU
28	3:13	PIS
30	12:00	ARI

NOV
Day	Time	Sign
1	18:23	TAU
3	23:01	GEM
6	2:30	CAN
8	5:18	LEO
10	7:58	VIR
12	11:23	LIB
14	16:39	SCO
17	0:42	SAG
19	11:39	CAP
22	0:11	AQU
24	11:59	PIS
26	21:05	ARI
29	2:58	TAU

DEC
Day	Time	Sign
1	6:22	CAN
3	8:31	LEO
5	10:40	VIR
7	13:42	LIB
9	18:13	SCO
12	0:34	SAG
14	9:04	CAP
16	19:48	AQU
19	8:12	PIS
21	20:35	ARI
24	6:45	TAU
26	13:15	GEM
28	16:15	CAN
30	17:05	LEO

—1975—

JAN
Day	Time	Sign
1	17:32	VIR
3	19:21	LIB
5	23:00	SCO
8	6:39	SAG
10	15:58	CAP
13	3:03	AQU
15	15:23	PIS
18	4:03	ARI
20	15:21	TAU
22	23:23	GEM
25	3:20	CAN
27	4:00	LEO
29	3:14	VIR
31	3:13	LIB

FEB
Day	Time	Sign
2	5:53	SCO
4	12:10	SAG
6	21:42	CAP
9	9:16	AQU
11	21:45	PIS
14	10:22	ARI
16	22:09	TAU
19	7:35	GEM
21	13:18	CAN
23	15:13	LEO
25	14:37	VIR
27	13:38	LIB

MAR
Day	Time	Sign
1	14:33	SCO
3	19:05	SAG
6	3:39	CAP
8	15:09	AQU
11	3:49	PIS
13	16:18	ARI
16	3:52	TAU
18	13:43	GEM
20	20:48	CAN
23	0:31	LEO
25	1:21	VIR
27	0:51	LIB
29	1:08	SCO
31	4:09	SAG

APR
Day	Time	Sign
2	11:08	CAP
4	21:45	AQU
7	10:17	PIS
9	22:44	ARI
12	9:53	TAU
14	19:14	GEM
17	2:27	CAN
19	7:14	LEO
21	9:42	VIR
23	10:41	LIB
25	11:39	SCO
27	14:20	SAG
29	20:08	CAP

MAY
Day	Time	Sign
2	5:34	AQU
4	17:34	PIS
7	6:03	ARI
9	17:03	TAU
12	1:44	GEM
14	8:08	CAN
16	12:38	LEO
18	15:45	VIR
20	18:05	LIB
22	20:25	SCO
23	23:51	SAG
27	5:31	CAP
29	14:09	AQU

JUN
Day	Time	Sign
1	1:32	PIS
3	14:01	ARI
6	1:19	TAU
8	9:49	GEM
10	15:21	CAN
12	18:45	LEO
14	21:11	VIR
16	23:41	LIB
19	2:59	SCO
21	7:34	SAG
23	13:56	CAP
25	22:33	AQU
28	9:33	PIS
30	22:02	ARI

JUL
Day	Time	Sign
3	9:54	TAU
5	18:58	GEM
8	0:23	CAN
10	2:50	LEO
12	3:55	VIR
14	5:21	LIB
16	8:23	SCO
18	13:32	SAG
20	20:46	CAP
23	5:56	AQU
25	16:58	PIS
28	5:27	ARI
30	17:53	TAU

AUG
Day	Time	Sign
2	4:02	GEM
4	10:17	CAN
6	12:44	LEO
8	12:53	VIR
10	12:51	LIB
12	14:30	SCO
14	18:59	SAG
17	2:25	CAP
19	12:09	AQU
21	23:32	PIS
24	12:02	ARI
27	0:45	TAU
29	11:53	GEM
31	19:35	CAN

SEP
Day	Time	Sign
2	23:08	LEO
4	23:29	VIR
6	22:38	LIB
8	22:46	SCO
11	1:41	SAG
13	8:11	CAP
15	17:51	AQU
18	5:32	PIS
20	18:07	ARI
23	6:43	TAU
25	18:13	GEM
28	3:07	CAN
30	8:20	LEO

OCT
Day	Time	Sign
2	10:03	VIR
4	9:39	LIB
6	9:09	SCO
8	10:35	SAG
10	15:29	CAP
13	0:10	AQU
15	11:40	PIS
18	0:20	ARI
20	12:43	TAU
22	23:51	GEM
25	8:57	CAN
27	15:20	LEO
29	18:47	VIR
31	19:55	LIB

NOV
Day	Time	Sign
2	20:07	SCO
4	21:10	SAG
7	0:45	CAP
9	7:59	AQU
11	18:42	PIS
14	7:17	ARI
16	19:38	TAU
19	6:14	GEM
21	14:36	CAN
23	20:48	LEO
26	1:04	VIR
28	3:48	LIB
30	5:37	SCO

DEC
Day	Time	Sign
2	7:33	SAG
4	10:58	CAP
6	17:12	AQU
9	2:52	PIS
11	15:06	ARI
14	3:39	TAU
16	14:12	GEM
18	21:49	CAN
21	2:54	LEO
23	6:28	VIR
25	9:27	LIB
27	12:28	SCO
29	15:53	SAG
31	20:16	CAP

LOVE SIGNS FOR BEGINNERS

—1976—

JAN
3	2:33	AQU
5	11:35	PIS
7	23:21	ARI
10	12:10	TAU
13	23:19	GEM
15	7:00	CAN
17	11:15	LEO
19	13:25	VIR
21	15:10	LIB
23	17:48	SCO
25	21:51	SAG
28	3:24	CAP
30	10:34	AQU

FEB
1	19:47	PIS
4	7:17	ARI
6	20:13	TAU
9	8:16	GEM
11	16:59	CAN
13	21:32	LEO
15	22:59	VIR
17	23:14	LIB
20	0:14	SCO
22	3:18	SAG
24	8:54	CAP
26	16:48	AQU
29	2:42	PIS

MAR
2	14:22	ARI
5	3:18	TAU
7	15:56	GEM
10	1:59	CAN
12	7:55	LEO
14	9:59	VIR
16	9:44	LIB
18	9:17	SCO
20	10:34	SAG
22	14:48	CAP
24	22:19	AQU
27	8:34	PIS
29	20:37	ARI

APR
1	9:34	TAU
3	22:15	GEM
6	9:06	CAN
8	16:36	LEO
10	20:16	VIR
12	20:54	LIB
14	20:14	SCO
16	20:15	SAG
18	22:43	CAP
21	4:47	AQU
23	14:28	PIS
26	2:37	ARI
28	15:37	TAU

MAY
1	4:05	GEM
3	14:53	CAN
5	23:09	LEO
8	4:21	VIR
10	6:39	LIB
12	7:03	SCO
14	7:04	SAG
16	8:31	CAP
18	13:02	AQU
20	21:27	PIS
23	9:07	ARI
25	22:07	TAU
28	10:22	GEM
30	20:39	CAN

JUN
2	4:37	LEO
4	10:21	VIR
6	14:00	LIB
8	15:58	SCO
10	17:07	SAG
12	18:45	CAP
14	22:31	AQU
17	5:43	PIS
19	16:32	ARI
22	5:21	TAU
24	17:37	GEM
27	3:29	CAN
29	10:39	LEO

JUL
1	15:46	VIR
3	19:34	LIB
5	22:33	SCO
8	1:05	SAG
10	3:49	CAP
12	7:53	AQU
14	14:36	PIS
17	0:40	ARI
19	13:11	TAU
22	1:40	GEM
24	11:39	CAN
26	18:19	LEO
28	22:23	VIR
31	1:13	LIB

AUG
2	3:55	SCO
4	7:03	SAG
6	10:54	CAP
8	15:57	AQU
11	23:00	PIS
13	8:49	ARI
15	21:05	TAU
18	9:54	GEM
20	20:34	CAN
23	3:31	LEO
25	7:04	VIR
27	8:42	LIB
29	10:05	SCO
31	12:28	SAG

SEP
2	16:29	CAP
4	22:20	AQU
7	6:11	PIS
9	16:18	ARI
12	4:30	TAU
14	17:32	GEM
17	5:07	CAN
19	13:11	LEO
21	17:16	VIR
23	18:28	LIB
25	18:34	SCO
27	19:21	SAG
29	22:13	CAP

OCT
2	3:49	AQU
4	12:10	PIS
6	22:50	ARI
9	0:14	TAU
11	11:11	GEM
14	0:14	CAN
16	12:24	LEO
18	21:49	VIR
21	3:25	LIB
23	5:17	SCO
25	4:49	SAG
27	5:55	CAP
29	10:05	AQU
31	17:53	PIS

NOV
3	4:46	ARI
5	17:23	TAU
8	6:21	GEM
10	18:28	CAN
13	4:36	LEO
15	11:46	VIR
17	15:34	LIB
19	16:32	SCO
21	16:03	SAG
23	16:03	CAP
25	18:30	AQU
28	0:47	PIS
30	11:01	ARI

DEC
2	23:41	TAU
5	12:38	GEM
8	0:21	CAN
10	10:12	LEO
12	17:55	VIR
14	23:13	LIB
17	2:01	SCO
19	2:54	SAG
21	3:12	CAP
23	4:48	AQU
25	9:36	PIS
27	18:32	ARI
30	6:43	TAU

—1977—

JAN
1	19:43	GEM
4	7:12	CAN
6	16:20	LEO
8	23:23	VIR
11	4:48	LIB
13	8:44	SCO
15	11:18	SAG
17	13:02	CAP
19	15:12	AQU
21	19:30	PIS
24	3:19	ARI
26	14:41	TAU
29	3:37	GEM
31	15:20	CAN

FEB
3	0:11	LEO
5	6:17	VIR
7	10:36	LIB
9	14:04	SCO
11	17:11	SAG
13	20:14	CAP
15	23:45	AQU
18	4:45	PIS
20	12:22	ARI
22	23:06	TAU
25	11:50	GEM
28	0:02	CAN

MAR
2	9:25	LEO
4	15:19	VIR
6	18:34	LIB
8	20:37	SCO
10	1:40	SAG
13	6:00	CAP
15	12:06	AQU
17	20:23	PIS
19	7:05	ARI
21	19:39	TAU
24	8:16	GEM
27	18:40	CAN
29	—	LEO

APR
3	1:25	VIR
5	4:39	LIB
7	5:40	SCO
9	6:08	SAG
11	7:40	CAP
13	11:24	AQU
15	17:49	PIS
18	2:52	ARI
20	14:02	TAU
23	2:37	GEM
25	15:25	CAN
28	2:43	LEO
30	10:52	VIR

MAY
2	16:24	SCO
4	15:59	SAG
6	15:54	CAP
8	18:00	AQU
10	23:39	PIS
13	8:29	ARI
15	20:04	TAU
18	8:50	GEM
20	21:35	CAN
23	9:13	LEO
25	18:31	VIR
28	0:28	LIB
30	2:57	SCO

JUN
1	2:54	SAG
3	2:07	CAP
5	2:44	AQU
7	6:35	PIS
9	14:34	ARI
12	1:56	TAU
14	14:50	GEM
17	3:28	CAN
19	14:53	LEO
22	0:29	VIR
24	7:35	LIB
26	11:42	SCO
28	13:02	SAG
30	12:48	CAP

JUL
2	12:56	AQU
4	15:31	PIS
6	22:03	ARI
9	21:15	TAU
11	9:50	GEM
14	5:58	CAN
16	13:09	LEO
19	18:13	VIR
21	21:04	LIB
24	22:15	SCO
27	23:04	SAG
29	—	CAP

AUG
1	1:23	AQU
3	6:54	PIS
5	16:18	ARI
8	4:29	TAU
10	17:04	GEM
13	3:57	CAN
15	12:26	LEO
17	18:49	VIR
19	23:35	LIB
22	3:03	SCO
24	5:30	SAG
26	7:41	CAP
28	10:46	AQU
30	16:11	PIS

SEP
2	0:52	TAU
4	12:27	GEM
7	1:03	CAN
9	12:14	LEO
11	20:34	VIR
14	2:07	LIB
16	5:45	SCO
18	8:28	SAG
20	11:04	CAP
22	14:12	AQU
25	0:26	PIS
27	7:34	ARI
29	16:53	TAU

OCT
1	20:33	GEM
4	9:09	CAN
6	20:58	LEO
9	5:59	VIR
11	11:29	LIB
13	14:11	SCO
15	15:27	SAG
17	16:51	CAP
19	19:36	AQU
22	0:26	PIS
24	7:34	ARI
26	16:53	TAU
29	4:08	GEM
31	16:40	CAN

NOV
3	5:03	LEO
5	15:17	VIR
7	21:51	LIB
10	0:42	SCO
12	1:03	SAG
14	0:50	CAP
16	2:00	AQU
18	5:58	PIS
20	13:13	ARI
22	23:35	TAU
25	10:48	GEM
27	23:20	CAN
30	11:53	LEO

DEC
2	23:05	VIR
5	7:18	LIB
7	11:33	SCO
10	12:22	SAG
12	11:26	CAP
14	10:59	AQU
17	13:09	PIS
19	19:11	ARI
22	4:54	TAU
24	16:51	GEM
27	5:30	CAN
29	17:52	LEO
30	5:13	VIR

LOVE SIGNS FOR BEGINNERS

—1978—

JAN
Day	Time	Sign
1	14:31	LIB
3	20:35	SCO
5	23:03	SAG
7	22:55	CAP
9	22:50	AQU
12	3:05	PIS
14	11:30	ARI
16	18:56	TAU
19	23:06	GEM
21	11:50	CAN
24	0:02	LEO
26	10:56	VIR
28	20:08	LIB
31	3:04	SCO

FEB
Day	Time	Sign
2	7:13	SAG
4	8:50	CAP
6	9:04	AQU
8	9:47	PIS
10	12:56	ARI
12	19:50	TAU
15	6:24	GEM
17	18:56	CAN
20	7:10	LEO
22	17:39	VIR
25	2:03	LIB
27	8:28	SCO

MAR
Day	Time	Sign
1	13:02	SAG
3	15:58	CAP
5	17:51	AQU
7	19:45	PIS
9	23:08	ARI
12	5:18	TAU
14	14:48	GEM
17	2:49	CAN
19	15:12	LEO
22	1:49	VIR
24	9:41	LIB
26	15:01	SCO
28	18:37	SAG
30	21:23	CAP

APR
Day	Time	Sign
2	0:05	AQU
4	3:20	PIS
6	7:51	ARI
8	14:21	TAU
10	23:27	GEM
13	10:59	CAN
15	23:30	LEO
18	10:44	VIR
20	18:53	LIB
22	23:39	SCO
25	2:00	SAG
27	3:27	CAP
29	5:28	AQU

MAY
Day	Time	Sign
1	9:00	PIS
3	14:27	ARI
5	21:52	TAU
8	7:18	GEM
10	18:41	CAN
13	7:17	LEO
15	19:15	VIR
18	4:24	LIB
20	9:39	SCO
22	11:31	SAG
24	11:41	CAP
26	12:10	AQU
28	14:36	PIS
30	19:52	ARI

JUN
Day	Time	Sign
2	3:50	TAU
4	13:53	GEM
7	1:30	CAN
9	14:07	LEO
12	2:35	VIR
14	12:55	LIB
16	19:28	SCO
18	22:03	SAG
20	21:57	CAP
22	21:07	AQU
24	21:57	PIS
27	1:53	ARI
29	9:21	TAU

JUL
Day	Time	Sign
1	19:37	GEM
4	7:33	CAN
6	20:13	LEO
9	8:44	VIR
11	19:48	LIB
14	3:47	SCO
16	7:50	SAG
18	8:33	CAP
20	7:41	AQU
22	7:26	PIS
24	9:46	ARI
26	15:50	TAU
29	1:31	GEM
31	13:28	CAN

AUG
Day	Time	Sign
3	2:10	LEO
5	14:29	VIR
8	1:30	LIB
10	10:11	SCO
12	15:43	SAG
14	18:03	CAP
16	18:15	AQU
18	18:04	PIS
20	19:29	ARI
23	0:06	TAU
25	8:31	GEM
27	19:59	CAN
30	8:40	LEO

SEP
Day	Time	Sign
1	20:46	VIR
4	7:15	LIB
6	15:38	SCO
8	21:39	SAG
11	1:20	CAP
13	3:09	AQU
15	4:09	PIS
17	5:50	ARI
19	9:43	TAU
21	16:56	GEM
24	3:31	CAN
26	16:02	LEO
29	4:11	VIR

OCT
Day	Time	Sign
1	14:17	LIB
3	21:48	SCO
6	3:07	SAG
8	6:52	CAP
10	9:42	AQU
12	12:12	PIS
14	15:06	ARI
16	19:22	TAU
19	2:05	GEM
21	11:52	CAN
24	0:04	LEO
26	12:32	VIR
28	22:51	LIB
31	5:53	SCO

NOV
Day	Time	Sign
2	10:03	SAG
4	12:40	CAP
6	15:04	AQU
8	18:06	PIS
10	22:11	ARI
13	3:35	TAU
15	10:45	GEM
17	20:16	CAN
20	8:09	LEO
22	20:57	VIR
25	8:07	LIB
27	15:39	SCO
29	19:23	SAG

DEC
Day	Time	Sign
1	20:44	SAG
3	21:35	CAP
5	23:36	AQU
8	3:40	PIS
10	9:50	ARI
12	17:54	TAU
15	3:50	GEM
17	15:37	CAN
20	4:34	LEO
22	16:40	VIR
25	1:32	LIB
27	6:07	SCO
29	7:15	SAG
31	6:53	CAP

—1979—

JAN
Day	Time	Sign
2	7:08	PIS
4	9:41	ARI
6	15:17	TAU
8	23:42	GEM
11	10:14	CAN
13	22:16	LEO
16	11:10	VIR
18	23:40	LIB
21	9:51	SCO
23	16:08	SAG
25	18:27	CAP
27	18:12	AQU
29	17:25	PIS
31	18:11	ARI

FEB
Day	Time	Sign
2	22:03	TAU
5	5:33	GEM
7	16:06	CAN
10	17:18	LEO
12	17:18	VIR
15	16:12	LIB
17	5:37	SCO
19	16:12	SAG
22	23:51	CAP
24	4:00	AQU
26	5:12	PIS
28	4:52	ARI

MAR
Day	Time	Sign
2	7:09	TAU
4	12:58	GEM
6	22:34	CAN
9	10:47	LEO
11	23:42	VIR
14	11:42	LIB
16	21:49	SCO
19	5:38	SAG
21	10:56	CAP
23	13:52	AQU
25	15:04	PIS
27	15:47	ARI
29	17:36	TAU
31	22:08	GEM

APR
Day	Time	Sign
3	6:24	CAN
5	17:58	LEO
8	6:52	VIR
10	18:45	LIB
13	4:16	SCO
15	11:18	SAG
17	16:23	CAP
19	20:02	AQU
21	22:41	PIS
24	0:51	ARI
26	3:27	TAU
28	7:48	GEM
30	15:11	CAN

MAY
Day	Time	Sign
3	1:56	LEO
5	14:41	VIR
8	2:48	LIB
10	12:10	SCO
12	18:25	SAG
14	22:25	CAP
17	1:26	AQU
19	4:18	PIS
21	7:30	ARI
23	11:20	TAU
25	17:18	GEM
27	23:23	CAN
30	10:08	LEO

JUN
Day	Time	Sign
1	22:41	VIR
4	11:12	LIB
6	21:05	SCO
9	3:15	SAG
11	6:23	CAP
13	7:56	AQU
15	9:56	PIS
17	12:52	ARI
19	17:18	TAU
21	23:23	GEM
24	7:24	CAN
26	17:47	LEO
29	6:14	VIR

JUL
Day	Time	Sign
1	19:08	LIB
4	5:57	SCO
6	12:56	SAG
8	16:07	CAP
10	16:59	AQU
12	18:57	PIS
14	22:43	ARI
17	5:00	TAU
19	13:40	GEM
22	0:30	CAN
24	13:01	LEO
27	2:06	VIR
29	13:46	LIB

AUG
Day	Time	Sign
2	22:05	SAG
5	2:23	CAP
7	3:28	AQU
9	3:05	PIS
11	3:10	ARI
13	5:21	TAU
15	10:41	GEM
17	19:17	CAN
20	6:28	LEO
22	19:11	VIR
25	8:13	LIB
27	20:12	SCO
30	5:39	SAG

SEP
Day	Time	Sign
1	11:34	CAP
3	13:59	AQU
5	14:03	PIS
7	13:29	ARI
9	14:12	TAU
11	17:54	GEM
14	1:27	CAN
16	12:25	LEO
19	1:15	VIR
21	14:11	LIB
24	1:54	SCO
26	11:36	SAG
28	18:40	CAP
30	22:49	AQU

OCT
Day	Time	Sign
3	0:23	PIS
5	0:28	ARI
7	0:45	TAU
9	3:07	GEM
11	9:12	CAN
13	19:12	LEO
16	7:51	VIR
18	20:44	LIB
21	8:02	SCO
23	17:09	SAG
26	0:11	CAP
28	5:16	AQU
30	8:29	PIS

NOV
Day	Time	Sign
1	10:09	ARI
3	11:16	TAU
5	13:25	GEM
7	18:23	CAN
10	3:14	LEO
12	15:20	VIR
15	4:16	LIB
17	15:29	SCO
19	23:56	SAG
22	6:01	CAP
24	10:37	AQU
26	14:17	PIS
28	17:17	ARI
30	19:54	TAU

DEC
Day	Time	Sign
2	23:02	GEM
5	4:01	CAN
7	12:09	LEO
9	23:33	VIR
12	12:29	LIB
15	0:08	SCO
17	8:36	SAG
19	13:55	CAP
21	17:13	AQU
23	19:50	PIS
25	22:40	ARI
28	2:08	TAU
30	6:32	GEM

— 115 —

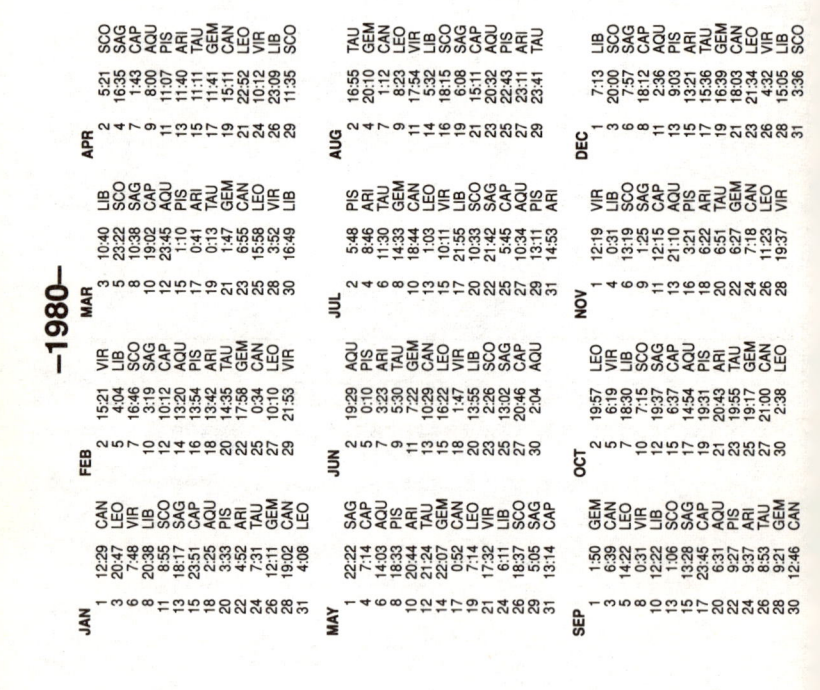

LOVE SIGNS FOR BEGINNERS

—1980—

JAN
1	12:29	CAN	
3	20:47	LEO	
6	7:48	VIR	
8	20:38	LIB	
11	8:55	SCO	
13	18:17	SAG	
15	23:51	CAP	
18	2:25	AQU	
20	3:33	PIS	
22	4:52	ARI	
24	7:31	TAU	
26	12:11	GEM	
28	19:02	CAN	
31	4:08	LEO	

FEB
2	15:21	VIR	
5	4:04	LIB	
7	16:46	SCO	
10	3:19	SAG	
12	10:12	CAP	
14	13:20	AQU	
16	13:54	PIS	
18	13:42	ARI	
20	14:35	TAU	
22	17:58	GEM	
25	0:34	CAN	
27	10:10	LEO	
29	21:53	VIR	

MAR
3	10:40	LIB	
5	23:22	SCO	
8	10:38	SAG	
10	19:02	CAP	
12	23:45	AQU	
15	1:10	PIS	
17	0:41	ARI	
19	0:13	TAU	
21	1:47	GEM	
23	6:55	CAN	
25	15:58	LEO	
28	3:52	VIR	
30	16:49	LIB	

APR
2	5:21	SCO	
4	16:35	SAG	
7	1:43	CAP	
9	8:00	AQU	
11	11:07	PIS	
13	11:40	ARI	
15	11:11	TAU	
17	11:41	GEM	
19	15:11	CAN	
21	22:52	LEO	
24	10:12	VIR	
26	23:09	LIB	
29	11:35	SCO	

MAY
1	22:22	SAG	
4	7:14	CAP	
6	14:03	AQU	
8	18:33	PIS	
10	20:44	ARI	
12	21:24	TAU	
14	22:07	GEM	
17	0:52	CAN	
19	7:14	LEO	
21	17:32	VIR	
24	6:11	LIB	
26	18:37	SCO	
29	5:05	SAG	
31	13:14	CAP	

JUN
2	19:29	AQU	
5	0:10	PIS	
7	3:23	ARI	
9	5:30	TAU	
11	7:22	GEM	
13	10:29	CAN	
15	16:22	LEO	
18	1:47	VIR	
20	13:55	LIB	
23	2:26	SCO	
25	13:02	SAG	
27	20:46	CAP	
30	2:04	AQU	

JUL
2	5:48	PIS	
4	8:46	ARI	
6	11:30	TAU	
8	14:33	GEM	
10	18:44	CAN	
13	1:03	LEO	
15	10:11	VIR	
17	21:55	LIB	
20	10:33	SCO	
22	21:42	SAG	
25	5:45	CAP	
27	10:34	AQU	
29	13:11	PIS	
31	14:53	ARI	

AUG
2	16:55	TAU	
4	20:10	GEM	
7	1:12	CAN	
9	8:23	LEO	
11	17:54	VIR	
14	5:32	LIB	
16	18:15	SCO	
19	6:08	SAG	
21	15:11	CAP	
23	20:32	AQU	
25	22:43	PIS	
27	23:11	ARI	
29	23:41	TAU	

SEP
1	1:50	GEM	
3	6:39	CAN	
5	14:22	LEO	
8	0:31	VIR	
10	12:22	LIB	
13	1:06	SCO	
15	13:28	SAG	
17	23:45	CAP	
20	6:31	AQU	
22	9:27	PIS	
24	9:37	ARI	
26	8:53	TAU	
28	9:21	GEM	
30	12:46	CAN	

OCT
2	19:57	LEO	
5	6:19	VIR	
7	18:30	LIB	
10	7:15	SCO	
12	19:37	SAG	
15	6:37	CAP	
17	14:54	AQU	
19	19:31	PIS	
21	20:43	ARI	
23	19:55	TAU	
25	19:17	GEM	
27	21:00	CAN	
30	2:38	LEO	

NOV
1	12:19	VIR	
4	0:31	LIB	
6	13:19	SCO	
9	1:25	SAG	
11	12:15	CAP	
13	21:10	AQU	
16	3:21	PIS	
18	6:22	ARI	
20	6:51	TAU	
22	6:27	GEM	
24	7:18	CAN	
26	11:23	LEO	
28	19:37	VIR	

DEC
1	7:13	LIB	
3	20:00	SCO	
6	7:57	SAG	
8	18:12	CAP	
11	2:36	AQU	
13	9:03	PIS	
15	13:21	ARI	
17	15:36	TAU	
19	16:39	GEM	
21	18:03	CAN	
23	21:34	LEO	
26	4:32	VIR	
28	15:05	LIB	
31	3:36	SCO	

— 116 —

FURTHER READING

Birbeck, Lyn, *Sun, Moon and Planet Signs*, Bloomsbury Press, 1992
Golder, Carole, *Love Lives*, Piatkus
Golder, Carole, *Seductive Art of Astrology*, Piatkus
Greene, Liz, *Astrology for Lovers*, Aquarian Press, 1993
Harvey, Charles and Suzi, *Sun Sign, Moon Sign*, Aquarian Press, 1994
Reynolds, Carolyn, *The Book of Lovers*, Llewellyn, 1992
Saunders, Jeraldine, *Signs of Love*, Llewellyn, 1991
Stone, Pauline, *Relationships, Astrology and Karma*, Aquarian Press, 1992
Thornton, Penny, *Suns and Lovers*, Aquarian Press, 1986
Thornton, Penny, *Synastry: A Comprehensive Guide to the Astrology of Relationships*, Aquarian Press, 1983
Zolar, *Zolar's Starmates*, Simon and Schuster, 1992